FORCE
FIELD
WIZARDRY
How To Develop Instinctive Thinking

BY

**JOSEPH W. GRAHAM, Ph. D.,
BUSINESS ADMINISTRATION**

Founder of *The Black Chair Series*.

Today, he's the author of over 100 books/eBooks such as *Master The Art of Context Thinking, The 11 Golden Principles of Context Thinking, Sense & Respond: Thinking at a 24/7 Pace, Thinking Quadrant: How to Think on Your Feet Even When You're Sitting, Strategic Foresight*, and many others, published worldwide.

COPYRIGHT

Columbia, SC 29223

Knowing when and where to place things is easy. Mindfulness of where things can be placed and maintained is hard. Movement rates are key to knowing when to take risks. One wins in life only by taking risks.

TABLE OF CONTENTS

Preface

We are excited to offer this extraordinary book loaded with great features, plus it comes with real-time value. Meticulous in its detail. Treat yourself to a wonderful mind-blowing experience in the comfort of your own home/office. Be mentally sharp and quick to see the meaning of new information. Grasp situations by understanding the scope and range, the before and after, of plans, things. To truly see, you will need to look for *FORCE FIELD WIZARDRY* that reveals Itself as *economy, elegance, and simplicity* (EES).

Smarter thinking in real time is just the beginning. Artificial Intelligent technologies are now enabling individuals to become increasingly intelligent. The goal is to obtain a balance, an internal guidance system, for minimizing disruptions of capabilities and uncertainties of requirements planning by optimizing forecasting and reporting when you are off track and need to self-correct to get back on track. Requirements planning is a big problem for many organizations and people, but by using intelligent thinking, one can tap into and leverage AI to see the variations and trends in process to improve its bottom-line results by cutting distribution costs and reducing errors. This would make the process and system more resilient.

This book is the benchmark of modern thinking; FORCE FIELD WIZARDRY. You've found the one you've been looking for. The one you dreamed about, the quintessential book that speaks volumes about you, uncompromising, individuality, passion for excellent standards that are far above the ordinary that makes this single book the one to own.

We are faced with the same conflicted problems. The everyday problems of living as individuals and in a complex society. Our goal at the outset is to listen, become aware of, see, make sense of, and understand the interrelated unity or discover the one element or factor that unites all between the problems, systems, and processes, however diverse they might be and at the same time summarize our conversations in themes and effectively apply what we think we know to guide and support you.

But where is the starting point of our conversations? Where do we begin?

You want to achieve the crucial, *instinctual* breakthrough of *insight*. This insight allows you to no longer either be a thinker or prophet because you have managed to tap into what only a few manage to achieve, tapped into your full potential. You do this as you attempt to simplify and clarify ends in the presence of silence and of the game of life. But more importantly, where do you concentrate your *efforts* that will allow you to a vantage point that is above the noise/struggles of life?

Be aware of the fact that the problems do not simply disappear once they have been identified. And they don't because we have too much at stake in reinstating them. We look to sharpen awareness of or discern what's going on in other works/arenas. This makes you question your assumptions about life. It confirms our conventional ways of seeing and talking about moments you experience.

Our relation to the people, places, and things we come across in our lives is a mysterious one. We have great loves in our lives. Some people we fall in love with because they said the right things at the right time; other places and things are lost to us forever because we were not ready for them when they crossed our paths and chance does not bring us into contact with them a second time.

With these encounters which have meant most to us there is nearly always the sense of an inexhaustible richness, of something we have to grow up to and into, and which will never reveal itself entirely. Nevertheless, with such encounters, there is always the sense of an instinctive understanding, an essential moment of awareness that what is lacking is really only the ability to make such understanding fully conscious that one feels a sense of infinitely closeness or distance at the same time. The intersection of happiness, destiny, and value of your worth/work comes together in a moment of perfection. The encounter with something that helps to release something beautiful within you that can be discerned from far-off horizons.

What is the source of your motivation, desire to know, feel? If freedom and self-fulfillment is the goal, what still stands as you get close to your center/core? It is this place that one will capture the moving moments encountered in one's life and then re-image them, identifying the high points of your expectation, using your imagination. It's not how to respond to what you imagine, but how to relate that response to the rest of one's life.

It is vitally important to concentrate power at the decisive point to influence superior or smaller force. Look for, anticipate, and shine your light on the little details of your capabilities and mistakes, then take a decisive moment, when a mental spark of insight or It arrives to counter your mistakes before they distract you. It is composed of vital processes and gives up the most intimate secrets of life. This impactful action reduces or eliminates the clouds and **reveals** the true essence of what you seek.

The clouds happen when there is a difference between what you know and don't know. The clouds are influenced by nearby bodies given the conditions and situations. Understanding is achieved by being aware of the total story, your position within the story, delivery times, and asking if the process within yourself is flexible, resilient, and optimized.

What I've discovered is that there is a secret essence within each of us; a rhythm, a flow, that must be synchronized. This instinctive rhythm must harmonize using the principle of non-linear weighted center of gravity within a contextual framework that allow you to think without thinking and to know without knowing.

Within the non-linear weighted center of gravity and contextual framework are critical timelines where coordination, de-conflicting, and tailoring, proportioning of requirements to capabilities takes place that leads to success or failure.

This book is what I've observed over my 56 years being on this planet around the best intellectual, sophisticated thinkers at their craft/work.

This comprehensive book is wake-up call for all people who desire to use FORCE FIELD WIZARDRY for success.

How do you effectively develop your

thinking to fully understand how to

instinctively process real-time information in a complex environment on a dynamic planet? Imagine this, by desiring to be so by enhancing your thinking method by using FORCE FIELD WIZARDRY as a strategy of layered/relational networked geometry/spatial projection of people and *fluid flow distribution* that allows exponential growth in flexibility, precision, and coordination to *anticipate* and be *creative, effective* and *resilient* in any conditions. Believing this, by the time you finish this book, you'll know how to get started and why!

Use FORCE FIELD WIZARDRY in any situation where you can be conscious of and track and control everything about what's going on around you, that you can't be lost in your own world-view, and can anticipate and have a successful outcome by shaping and influencing conditions by *what is* and *ought to be*. Most stuff does not work because people tend to not do what they ought to do. They do not understand their responsibilities. Briefly, this book is intended to show the reader the broad lay/lines of the land instead of the details, and for independent thinking instead of rote memorization, the general shape of the systems, the relations between them, and a way to communicate the value of what you see, feel, hear, and think.

Many of you have gone through the conventional schools and might have a hard time imagining that you can learn from a short unconventional approach to learning from a book. Let me reassure you that you can learn from this book, defy logic, and begin to think, know, and understand at another level; improving your imaginative wisdom and brain power.

The mindset revealed in this book incorporates the secrets held by only a select few over the centuries – and will allow you to amass money and wealth because you will have a deep understanding and a way to simply report about how things truly work and you will become that work of outstanding artistry, skill, or workmanship.

INTRODUCTION

As of this moment, your life will never be the same. When you read this book on FORCE FIELD WIZARDRY, you made a choice that will cost you time and energy. Why did you choose this book? You might have been prompted or driven by the cover design or your life experiences may have led you to this book, which I think is one of the most valuable books you could read. That's right. On the pages that follow within this book, you may find the very timely answer you have been looking for your entire life. It can provide you the key insight you have been seeking for years or give your life a profound meaning for things you did not even know you wanted, perhaps your entire life.

In this book, which is a special book, I am going to answer your questions so you will easily know how I do my stuff, why, when, where, and anything else when it comes to insider stuff to tapping into and developing brain power.

I should not reveal or share the secret knowledge told to me by a very successful person, but if you can count to 1, 2, 3…remember A, B, C, and maybe heard of the story of Black and White, you will see how easy it is to use these essential secret processes to make your life heightened, deeper, richer, and better.

These treasured secrets, uncovered in this great read, I will give you for free or for a fantastic small fee that only a small select few will take a chance to purchase this book.

You are one of those Select Few. Use these secrets to build your personal library for successful deeper thinking and living. You will be able to discern the season and time to use your skills to educate, inform, advance understanding, and share knowledge. Once exposed to this knowledge, you will be changed with each reading as essential truths are revealed.

You can use this book however you want to, start at the beginning or jump around as you desire and just start reading. This book is designed to engage your mind and get you thinking, using prescience to see far ahead to new solutions, about developing thoughts and possibilities you might have never thought of before, like developing and training your eye to see details and taste, and stopping and thinking about what lies behind your perceptions of people, places, and things because your mind IS sharper than you think.

So, use this book carefully, it contains great secrets, shared over the centuries and it has come down to me and now to you.   Don't let the secrets fall in the wrong hands, guard them and they will honor you with their staying power.

Now, the driving theme for this book is the question, **how to leverage FORCE FIELD WIZARDRY at the cutting-edge of success?** We will answer that question in a profound way in this book. FORCE FIELD WIZARDRY consists of three areas that will jump out at you at the right moment and that will be discussed throughout this book:

(1)   Hold the necessary sight alignment and make adjustments to grasp the situation

(2)   See a number of positions and instantly judge all the advantages from known positions

(3)   Master of non-linear time, space, and mass (concentration)

This practical book provides next-step insights for mastering the art of FORCE FIELD WIZARDRY that allows one to anticipate and be resourceful in a given situation in any environment by gaining a deeper understanding of the relationships of capabilities that underpin things. You will be able to strike a rock and bring forth the hidden secrets within these sentences. I hope this book proves useful to several kinds of reader. This book focuses on on-going self-development to expand your thinking beyond your own experience and education to give you an enhanced, holistic look and broader, reflective perspective in time and space. It's an eye-opening, hands-on, look at how to master the aspects of the applications that go into anticipating circumstances and determining desired and successful outcomes. It will help you when you have too many different incoming signals interacting in unexpected ways causing growing problems. It will help you use mind bets to achieve results. Some beautiful insights and results will arrive with staggering suddenness, while others may take years to show up and be laid bare.

It is my goal to woo you and provide a compelling and revised way of thinking about how to increase visual depth using exponential and spatial thinking that is happening as a result of converging exponential advances in technology. You can use the whole spectrum tools in this book to integrate and control any environment by learning how to use FORCE FIELD WIZARDRY to sense how to know what to do next and why doing it is important to increase the velocity of resources across time, space, and function in the right amount, at the right place, using speed, connection, and access to information, while reducing risks.

Yes. I've used distributed logistics or distribution management, because it is what I know best to illustrate my point, and if you stay awake as I'm using my example, you will see the subtle, universal changes you are looking for. The business manager is unable to handle problems due to disruptive cycle and complexities in intermediaries. Basically, logistics involve the distribution of goods from point of origin to point of destination. It is the practical art of moving armies and keeping them supplied. The assistance of transportation management will also be required to maintain lead-time from procurement of goods to end-customer delivery. So, my example using FORCE FIELD WIZARDRY will show and give you the best expertise as it is relating to strategic and operational logistics and transportation planning management support within a field of supply chain management to solve operational logistics problems.

Let me advise you, get a ring-side seat, for you are about to be INTELLIGENT

21

SUPPLY CHAIN-ed, so that you will understand how to support your needs with best practices to optimize your solutions.

I have designed this book in a way that you will learn about underpinnings of the levels of priority, domain, threat, power, and their significance and weights. There are **three vertical triangulated domains and levels** that you will work with are on a *strategic, operational, or tactical level*.

You will be trying to determine when **a shift or nuance** on one level influences/impacts or shifts actions on a new or old level. Domains are on a Physical level, Cognitive level, or Moral level (Is it ethical?) What are threats? Are they a local, regional, or global threat? What are impacts the elements of National Power – Political, Military,

Economic, Social, Intellectual, and Influence? What are the impacts of "DOTMLPF Spectrum" – which stands for "Doctrine, Organization, Training, Materiel, Leadership & Education, Personnel, and Facilities? What are the impacts of unknown or unanticipated inputs?

Thus, you will learn to take the three vertical levels and integrate them with **horizontal triangulated levels** (traditional linear thinking that uses **action – reaction – and counteraction** as the basis of *seeing, thinking about, and then doing things* to create reality). You will come to look for and see that there is no natural harmony and unity between the horizontal and vertical levels. You will have learned how to know where you are at a point in time…identifying shifts in risks that require mitigation and friction points such as error, delays, misunderstandings. You will learn when good enough can defeat better and better can defeat superior depending on the skill and design.

I have explained as clearly as possible so you will get a current understanding and a **Sense of Operational Design:** a three area platform that empowers you to determine how far you can go, how fast you need to move within, and how long you need to sustain yourself in order to optimize performance. The three key areas are operational reach/depth (determines how far you need go), operational tempo/rate (determines how fast), and Operational Sustainment/Direction (determines how long you need to stay in a location and sustain systems). All three elements provide you with the sense of the operational design. The Operational design provides you with purpose, intention, and a desired outcome.

This book will allow you to master the following skills:

- See through and size-up different situations quickly and come to a single solution repeatedly

- Understand how the world will work and move in the next 2 – 25 years

- Learn how to strategically think deeply and widely to improve decision-making skills and shift your decision calculus

- Know form follows function

- Identify six rules of life that are fixed in all situations

- Learn the priority of the rules of life that must be followed for success

- Master getting the opposition to violate their rules or will

- Deal with growth while maintaining balance, confidence, and creativity

- How to ask questions, make good decisions, influence others, prioritize, and take risks

- Get an incremental edge needed to win in any environment

- Ask even better questions and reflect to make better decisions that lead to insight

- Handle and adapt to the speed and variety of changing environments

- Disconnect from the noise and sense deeply the decisive moment

- Use algorithms, data sets, indexes, and themes to see results

- In a machine-driven age driving by speed – use judgment, time, and perspective as your competitive edge

- Step back and think about time-tested sharper ideas and applications

- Expand your intellectual horizons by the power of suggestion

- How to master plan, delegate, recruit people, and report information

- Think Outside-The-Box in a multidisciplinary way exploring and intuiting the profound meaning of things

- Grasp principles and underlying processes and values at a glance

- Relate new problems to old solved problems over a range of situations

- Learn what something means and more specifically, what it means to you

The contents will help you gain a holistic understanding of the underpinnings of the planning art; that they are part of a much larger, more complex with the goal of reduction or shrinking of time-distance between **Strategic Geometry/ Locations and Lines of Communication**. These two points are the pillars of planning art and the sharper position. The common center that undergirds these pillars interests.

You will come to make sense of the global/international environment. Making sense means knowing movement rates at different levels and how to mitigate actions based upon identifying where you should focus your attention based upon known and unforeseen consumption rates and requirements to close the gap by shifting resources, increasing or decreasing requirements, and/or working to quickly recover processes that undergird support requirements.

The contents of this book can also be used as an intellectual guide when you need to make necessary course corrections as you navigate by leveraging sharper and sensored-networks to help change objective foundations of concentrated thought; which is based on simple and proven mathematics like calculus and geometry. With what I'm about to share with you, you will be able to analyze and sort out what's important and interesting as you put things into context, see new insights, and anticipate trends as the master of your own ship.

Now, what are the key questions that you should be asking yourself and steps you should be looking for to achieve your goals and objectives?

Shortly, you will see in this book that you must be able to lead from the center position using center of gravity which is a continuous process throughout events. The center of gravity can change during the course of a tragic event and may not be apparent or readily discernible.

For example, just think, the dinosaur has long disappeared from the Earth, but the butterfly remains. What is the secret to its ability to sustain itself? I believe that when you understand the tools presented in this book, you can have a long successful personal and business life no matter the change that is around you.

In today's hectic world, it is essential for you to be able to confidently find out and communicate what to do as they adapt to quickly changing situations. This is by far the best practical book on achieving a FEEDBACK LOOP of success in your thinking life as you respond to those chaotic and **sharper** situations.

The smartest people of all times share <u>proven</u> systematic sequences they follow to discover their unique FORCE FIELD WIZARDRY that leads to strategies that leads to success.

My ideas are future oriented and as such are 25 years ahead of the rest of the world. They solve problems by showing the guiding principles, requirements, capabilities, processes, and way ahead when you are thinking and planning projects of strategic, operational, and tactical significance using the thinking with a phased approach.

A key question one needs to ask is: What are the key <u>indicators</u> that I'm seeing that support decision points/actions/ events/priorities by level and phases of operation and the execution rates of tasks?

We are now beginning to play the game of life in a sharper and exponential way. We have to learn to work together under new gold-plated, concentrated, modular, networked, sensored, scalable thought process that is presented in this simple and impactful book.

You must know how to successfully maneuvering between projects to gain insight into dynamic thought processes that will allow you to see indicators that show emerging requirements, delays, patterns, and trends.

Take a seat and learn some essential secrets of success – a collection of filters to make information into a network that has simple rules and how to use them.

Imagine this, you will awaken to an intelligent and invincible thinking that allows you to see how you can fly higher than an eagle and best navigate any chaotic environment, saving the valuable resource - **time**.

You will be able to find out what's important, determine a general direction, interpret metrics, and determine specific meaning in events. Sequencing is really about concentrated time management.

One can best navigate traditional and non-traditional environments by seeing and experiencing the big picture; knowing the overall big plan and direction and then be able to see the parallel decision points and weights of those points within daily requirements and actions. This will give you the concentrated awareness needed to ask, what is my sense of the situation and what's next? Am I doing the right things efficiently that will lead to my success with quickness, responsiveness, versatility, and adaptability?

Rare innovative and thinking people like, Einstein, Galileo, Michelangelo, Napoleon, and you already know that you must see what I call "Seeing the forest beyond the forest"; that is, be able to quickly see and imagine actions and impacts, *in real time*, of other entities upon your organization and you.

You must immediately respond with the right solution. Seeing the forest beyond the forest allows you the response time needed to get the right answer given a range of possibilities given locations and lines of communication.

For example, I've been writing books and books since 2001 and have seen that people's reading habits are declining; they say due to a lack of time. I used the concept of "seeing the forest beyond the forest" and applied it to publishing.

Since people say they don't have the time to read, I stepped back, concentrated, looked at other industries, and asked myself a simple and direct question; what can I do to help busy people create more time? What can I do to save readers hours of precious time and wasted dollars?

The answer came to me to publish an entire book on "One Page". It is similar to a summary, but with more information that can be used right away.

Here's an example at http://jgrahamenterprises.wix.com/onepag books

I could not have prepared the "One Page Books" without creatively seeing the forest beyond the forest. I successfully moved between the internal projects and projects of the other industries using what I discovered were best to create a new product. Imagine what it would be like if you applied this simple concept to what you are doing and see if you can come up with some breakthrough and beyond the forest outcomes.

Let me show you how to develop your ability to easily move between projects and integrate politics, economics, technology, justice, and social/religion so your efforts are amazingly successful.

Today I'm introducing key time-saving thinking concepts and tools that you can use to get the light-bulb to come on and stay on when learning to close gaps in your thinking.

This book is ultimately about **your thinking in time in environments that are within known contexts**, which you can use to have more success in your life. You can learn the art and science of central position thinking.

Principles, concepts, interests, and tools lay the foundation for your success on your journey from this moment forward. You will become way smarter than your friends, family members, and peers. The concepts and tools are very easy to use. You will be able to find immediate answers to questions that have time pressures attached to them.

Now Strategic Geometry and Lines of Communications determines figuring out how much stuff you should have at different places and times. This would be considered the main things that you want to accomplish. You would achieve these main things by sequencing products, services, and other things over time and space and developing your ability to think on your feet and multitask so that you can go farther, move faster, and stay longer supporting your interests.

You have to do a preparation of the environment; looking at terrain, lines of supply, locations of key roads, ports, units/people, and weather impacts.

You can use the central position to understand the mind of your opposition and force them to do things against its own rules of war and get off of their central position.

Thumb through this book and see the new and modern ideas presented.

We take a brief look at the balancing forces of diffusion of knowledge, center of gravity thinking, the impact of elements of national power, context thinking, and exponential thinking in mastering environments from the center of organizations; when you are not necessarily the leader of the organization, yet you are a leader within the organization.

What I'm about to show you is quite simple.

It's really simple.

Simplicity was one of Steve Job's principles when he developed products at Apple. As you continue to rush into your busy daily life doing multiple tasks, you need concepts and tools that can assist you in filtering through the vast amount of information that is being broadcasted. You desire to anticipate the right answer during the right time on problems that confront you.

You have to first establish the framework/foundation that allows you to integrate, sequence, and synchronize requirements, available capabilities, and see the processes that link the two. We will then show you how to use means available to you to see indicators that manifest as time-savings or power generation at decision points on your way to success.

This beautiful book will awaken you to the truth about those things that are around you, physical, intellectual, emotional, and spiritual, that can help you clearly see shades of meaning and the FORCE FIELD WIZARDRY of possibilities in everyday events. They help you to see the scripts and beyond the scripts one uses to make life more agreeable or less worrisome about everyday life.

We want you to have the perfect answer to fit your immediate need and have the priceless tools handy to save you some precious time.

It is our goal to help make your thinking life measurably greater, sweeter, fuller, and richer.

Let's begin…

Sequence 1: You first **Ask** the most important questions at all times…
Am I doing the right thing, things right, and where is the center or pillar, essential meaning, and purpose of what I'm seeing?

The answer to these questions allows you to see linear, geometric, and now exponential and spatial relations /relationships that are key to your understanding and insight. You will see the practical strategic lines, what's between and behind the lines (triggers and indicators), what is happening in the margins and gaps, and be able to talk to why things are important and why an action or principle works.

Your goal will be to take advantage of every circumstance by understanding their meaning and interpretation as they occur or likely to occur. You do this by learning…

How to master adapting to circumstances and determining successful outcomes by rethinking them at any given moment. This requires that you master the material in this book and learn to seek and **LISTEN** to the pearls of wisdom it presents. If you properly listen, you will develop the unique ability to make complex ideas and systems understandable. Key to your success is to ask the question **WHY** and be able to describe how the answer can be applied to improve performance.

CENTER OF GRAVITY 1

Triangulation to Master Time, Space, and
Mass (Concentration)

First things first. You must develop your
thinking skills using the non-linear concept
of center of gravity with the key information
for your life or industry. You have to know
what your centers are, and <u>triggers and
indicators</u> that show your decision points
and thinking vulnerabilities. This is done to
solve current issues and protect yourself
from a large amount of conflicting
information that is being created by others to
hide the real secret about how to obtain
power of thinking. Non-linear weighted
Center of Gravity is the essential ingredient

that binds tools, processes, and systems you are using in your organization and life. It helps to reduce risk and unnecessary duplication of efforts. It is the most important thing in warfare.

Now, let's define **Center of Gravity** to get a common understanding. Claude Von Clausewitz, a leading authority on Center of Gravity, felt that center of gravity is the "concentration" or "hub" of power.

Your curiosity, imagination, and insight will allow you to read and judge what is the center point or the focal point. Then you look at how things are categorized or grouped around the point. This allows you to ask (1) if there is a natural balance of resources? (2) what is the weight (importance) of the various components and

(3) will the foundations support those components?

In a nutshell, you have to concentrate on and see if the over-all picture and higher long-term advantages outweigh the short-term disadvantages and immediate short-term loss. You have to see value or worth, authorities, and rewards of the unmovable center.

All situations in life adhere to center of gravity. You will see and sense harmony and balance of when you awakened to the center of gravity of things. The geniuses of old, like Bach, Picasso, Plato, and Van Gogh, knew this to be true, and now you know it too.

Next, what counts is determining who has the ability to get things done. After that; knowing and understanding a thing and its implications on your situation. If you can understand the basic message and execute the tasks and steps that are associated with them, then you will succeed in seeing and communicating what and who counts.

Ok. With that out of the way, let's begin.

Now the Center of Gravity for navigating between projects are in knowing what will get the results you want fastest and in the quality you desire. Those things will bring increase with them and bring added benefits to you. They are the foundation or core of getting what you want from your efforts.

Below are areas you must focus on. Ask yourself these questions and listen for the answers to master any organization or industry.

1) What is the absolutely essential information needed?

2) What are the implications and ramifications of what I'm seeing?

3) What's the difference, or shades of meaning, in implications and ramifications?

4) Who else needs to have or know about what I have in front of me?

These four questions provide a symphony of answers for mastery in any organization or industry when used in concert with a center of gravity that will allow you to read between the lines.

Now, as an example, everyone should know about the distribution of wealth gap that exists in the world and its impact on them personally. Forces such as a nation's elements of power impact all of us.

Those geometric elements of power are a nation's *political, economic, technological, religious, and social institutions* that form the foundation of nations. Political deals with policy, economic deals with capital/income flow, technological deals with innovation, religious deals with moral standards and ethical values, and social deals with relationships among and between groups/classes.

All these elements of national power are *pillars* that impact the distribution of wealth or the lack there of. They are reasons for inequalities of wealth and income in countries around the world. To clearly see the impact of each element, you have to use the center of gravity to establish within yourself a point of view of things you are thinking about and seeing. You have to see the important aspects of how other people live and use the power generated from the elements and how to apply what you learn to everyday events.

It is not easy to see shades of meaning. Creatively seeing the shades of meaning obviously is not always easy. You have to experience things to truly know them. Reading what's presented here provides insight, but to truly know the material you have to take a look at your life and examine it to glean the wisdom from your life experiences. Examine your life to see the wisdom and insight that you already have.

For example, now, as you know, the distribution of wealth gap is increasing. Capital accumulation levels and rates are leading to further concentration of wealth into fewer hands; the One Percenters (1%). They have been increasing the wealth gap because they know how to build real wealth.

Real wealth is what I call capital/income ratio and flow mastery on an individual and group level. They have used their access to information in research programs to increase their training and skill levels about the rest of society. Capital here means a number of investment instruments and real estate that they own.

Income means the amount of effort they put into bringing in an income from labor. We will talk about this later as we talk about Context Thinking, but for now you should be aware of this fact.

The Wealthy simply know how to make their money work for themselves by ensuring that their **rate of return on capital** *exceeds* **the rate of growth** of Gross Domestic Product (GDP) or rate of growth of output and income of the economy.

You too can do the same.

You can do it by using the tools in this book to first get a firm understanding of what is really going on around you; getting the big picture and then acting on what you see by using the balancing forces of increasing your knowledge and using technology as your prime forecasting drivers where your eyes begin to hear and your ears begin to see.

You should also join with upstart groups of like-minded individuals who get your learning curve in a vertical position that allows you to learn things quicker.

Groups like network marketing companies are prime examples. Get in one today. Look for upstarts as they will provide the quickest way for many of you. Find one that focuses on education and literacy because knowledge is power. Use this power as a means to close the wealth gap. The diffusion of knowledge and investment in some training or skills program is key to your overall productivity and personal and professional growth. It will allow you to catch-up with the rich by getting access to information and sharing knowledge.

In sum, Non-linear weighted Center of Gravity is most useful at the level as an analytical tool to focus the effort against the enemy's strength while designing campaigns and operations to assist in analyzing friendly and adversary sources of strength as well as weaknesses and vulnerabilities. This analysis of non-linear weighted center of gravity is a continuous process throughout the operation because the centers of gravity can change during the course of an operation and may not be apparent or readily discernible. Identification of adversary weighted centers of gravity require detailed knowledge and understanding of how opponents organize, fight, and make decisions as well as their physical and psychological strengths and weaknesses. You must constantly monitor and concentrate on events that will cause the non-linear weighted centers of gravity to change and adjust your operations and actions accordingly in line with FORCE FIELD WIZARDRY.

CONTEXT AND FORCE FIELD

WIZARDRY 2

Sequence 2: **Seek** the many connections/ relationships and different ways (perspectives) by looking around you, paying attention to what you see, know, and do now and expect to see, know, do to influence the future.

We are all genius kids at heart and want to acquire deep smarts fast. We have been taught the principles of wisdom and context thinking since we were kids through our nursery rhymes. It is in your makeup called DNA. FORCE FIELD WIZARDRY allows to you collect data and put it into groups of like-minded information. This group of data can then be examined to see what patterns develop. What you see that fits together. These individual pieces of data or indicators become information that you can use thinking to begin to start to make into good knowledge.

Use Context Thinking to show the strategic geometry and wisdom needed as you use knowledge to make wise decisions and develop into successes. This action provides you with the new FORCE FIELD WIZARDRY tools to be successful in your thinking. It shows how even simple nursery rhymes reveal how to concentrate using context thinking and exponential thinking.

The following stories will provide you with an understanding of how to change your thinking and make you more confident in your choices.

Think back to when you were a child and had to learned the nursery rhyme, ***Jack and Jill.***

Jack and Jill went up the hill
To fetch a pail of water,
Jack fell down and broke his crown
And Jill came tumbling after.

This is a truly amazing and powerful story, but what makes it amazing and powerful?

The key things that make it amazing and powerful are they tell you about **FORCE FIELD WIZARDRY** or steps of context thinking used to make you think well. The story can be used as an example for you to become amazing and powerful when you think in terms of what you want, look for (foresight), understand now, and understand about your life.

Now Jack and Jill wanted to get some water so that they would not be thirsty or to cook some food so they could have a good life. They needed some water so they could know that their requirement for water was good. You will need to get water and other needed requirements to make your future good (strategic foresight). To make your future good, you have to see what is coming at you. You have to look both forward and backward (strategic hindsight) to get an understanding of what you see or what are the **"REQUIREMENTS"** for your life. Once you get the requirements, they help you with the whole problem of how to live life in a good way.

Now Jack and Jill went up the hill so they needed arms to carry the pails. Their arms represented that they needed the **"CAPABILITY"** or other people's capability to meet those "REQUIREMENTS" by understanding **"what"** the requirements were and **"who"** and **"where"** they are located to help you. The pail was designed to hold water and other things so they needed a strong pail built to last if they dropped it. The type of pail represents the **STANDARDS"** or value that guide Jack and Jill's goals in getting the water; the **"why"**.

Finally, Jack and Jill went up the hill that day to get water for that day. This represents the **"TIME"** factor it needs the most impact that is the **"when"** or "now" to know the desire in your life.

These four steps, **Requirements, Capabilities, Standards, and Timelines** can be used with purpose, intention, and a desired outcome to understand the way you think about anything in your life. Purpose points to requirements. Intention points to Capabilities. Desired outcome points to expectation about Standards and Time you want to accomplish a project. You will use these steps to understand new information that comes at you. Know how to size up relationships by measure, number, and weight and apply results by improvising and taking calculated risks and leveraging capabilities. It will allow you to use all data into easy ways so that it can begin to make sense to you. Any new data can be understood by use of these steps.

Context provides the framework to whatever you want to do in life. Context is based on the scarcity of resources - time, space, energy, etc. Context has four steps that we will cover shortly, but let's get a sound understanding of facts and assumptions.

Facts and assumptions resulting from the analysis are measured against a sculptured framework of four questions;

(1) **what is *required*,**

(2) **what is your *capability* to meet the requirement,**

(3) **what are the *standards* that are adhered to, and**

(4) **what is the *time* needed to get it done**?

Facts are statements of known data concerning the situation.
Assumptions are unknown data concerning the situation.

Many people have a problem identifying facts or just ignore facts, as if they are drunk with wine, because they don't' know how to properly apply them in a specific situation.

You should focus on and paint a picture by saying or asking "so what" when you encounter a fact.

What you should expect is to challenge assumptions.

You say to yourself, here is a fact about my situation and what does this fact mean? Is the fact a cause or effect, what are the pros or cons, is it a general to a specific fact or specific to a general fact, is the factual relationship a numerical or historical context?

A fact is real whether it is known or unknown. If a fact is known, you can measure it. If it is unknown, you can measure it by use of statistical probability or estimation of what you think you would see or where it is supposed to be located, or it could be an assumption.

Assumptions are suppositions or unknowns about the current or future situation, which are assumed true in the absence of facts, and are required to continue planning and thinking about your situation.

Assumptions should not wish away capabilities or assume capabilities. Your biggest enemy will be the unknown and assumptions. All assumptions not validated or eliminated in planning and thinking become risks in execution.

This captures all that you currently know and don't know in one place about your situation.

Next, be careful to build the framework in which you will leverage and execute the tasks needed to make your life successful.

The framework gives you boundaries from which you will operate.

Here you determine what right looks like projected in a future timeframe. If you can't see in the future, you can't take action and execute your power when stepping out in strategic leadership.

Frameworks allow you to see the culture of and focus on key people by identifying tasks, deciding what's important and what to *measure* and how to *measure* it, and at what acceptable risk to determine if you need help to achieve your desired results.

The following is a **Four (4) Step Framework** for you to use as you go through the decision-making process. As part of the process, the three basic questions you should always be able to ask and answer are:

- Where are you currently located?

- Why are you there?

- When, to where, and in what sequence do you move to ensure continuous improvement?

Know that there must be a range of acceptable performance for each answer. In power attainment, most of the time, it is not an all or none situation. So, when you ask questions, listen for the pain, desire, honor, and information that leads to understanding and specific answers that meet your purpose against the range of acceptable general answers.

Another example that reveals that we already know how to use these processes is shown by another nursery rhyme, *Goldilocks and The Three Bears.* It is a good example of the process of thinking better with Context Thinking. Goldilocks focused on the **Requirement** to find a comfortable seat and bed to rest. She tried out Papa Bear's chair, Mother Bear's Chair, and Baby Bair's Chair and saw that each had its own **Capabilities** to hold her. She also tried Papa Bear, Mother Bear, and Baby Bear Beds. Each was made out of different material, why? So that it would stand up under the weight of Papa Bear, Mama Bear, and Baby Bear. They had to have a type of **Standard** or they would fall to pieces. They had to go give a level of comfort. She found the Baby Bear's was just right and fell asleep to rest then which shows the **Time** to rest was now.

Finally, the story of the *Three Little Pigs*, show that you can sometimes get the **standards** wrong as the three pigs each built their houses out of different materials, but two of the three did not build it to withstand the Big Bad Wolf. The three little pigs were all aware of the **requirements** needed to keep the wolf out, but they thought different about what would be needed, **capability**, to keep him out. So, each pig made a different house of different strength. After the wolf blew down the first two pigs houses, the third pig's house was strong enough to keep the wolf out that day, which shows the **time**.

So, these nursery rhymes show that you already have the capability to use context thinking and have been taught them at as a child.

Use these simple steps to withstand the huffing and puffing of the Big Bad Wolf, find you a good place to rest when you get tired, and get you some needed water and food when you get thirsty in life.

Now always keep this in mind, these four steps of context thinking are based on your needs and wants at that particular time in your career and life, because you perceive things differently say when you were in your 20's versus your 50's.

In your 50s, you have sufficient mature understanding of faith, virtue, knowledge, temperance, patience, godliness, kindness, and love.

It is helpful to use *paired questioning* to get you through the process. You should be asking **"what and whom, where and when, and how and why"**.

These questions and steps can be used throughout your decision-making /problem-solving process to make the best decision about your situation. They will allow you to "Sense" or measure success, have a wide visibility: connectivity 24/7 with a global focus, "Control" events by having the right people and capabilities, shared awareness and processes, same standards of success, and to "Respond" to issues with rapid and precise response; with speed, reliability, visibility, and efficiency. These are all required for mastering your life and to help you increase your rate of return on capital and close wealth gaps that currently exists.

You can read more about context thinking in my book "Master the Art of Context Thinking. http://tinyurl.com/p3sw2q8

SCALING 3

Making the complex, not easier, but simpler.

Sequence 3: **Know:** Seeing the meaning of places, people, and things while grasping the grand drama requires imagination based on seeing levels and expectations.

Now that you have an understanding of Center of Gravity and Context Thinking, we can now sharpen your thinking by showing you how to use this new information to gain power for self and determine how to get things done when you are not "really" in charge of other organizations and agencies.

First, I define power as the ability to get things done. That ability is the "power hub" and it is supported by the pillars of politics, economics, technology, justice and social/religion.

From this hub, there extend the five pillars which make up the combined effect of power; which is the ability to get things done.

Each of the pillars represents a different function of power.

Critical to each function are the people who work there and their certifications/ training levels, their reach or influence, the equipment or tools that they use, the systems they put together to produce output, and the processes used to make the system work.

First and most important of these are the people. Of these people, there are select groups of people who have "real power"; they are the "go to" individuals who know how to frame and shape a battle Force Multiplier and make things happen for their organization. They risk-take on a breath-taking scaled when they have competing requirements and have to prioritize.

I witnessed this during my military career, when the U.S. Army would bring in a select group of people, usually Generals, to manage a military campaign. You could call them the "Dream Team". This Dream Team is located within all successful organizations and must be searched out when you encounter each pillar that supports the Power Hub. We will talk about my lessons learned from this "Dream Team" that was assembled to launch the Iraqi War and my insight into their thinking and decision-making process.

Second, their reach or influence is important in getting things done. They have the, it seems, natural ability to move easily between Power Centers and make things happen by looking for the gravitational pull in organizations. They are swift to hear, slow to speak, and slow to wrath. They know systems inside and out and know all the people who make them go.

They understand how to work a room when they need information and migrate comfortably between the separate levels of business, government, and even the arts. They *integrate*, for example, Federal, State, and Local Governments and Commercial Entities into one fluid organization within their mind; getting a clear understanding of the Interagency processes. People on the different levels respect them. It is gained because they are honest, accessible individuals and communicative with others; plus, they are not easily dismissed because of their knowledge of what right looks like. They know the way and their actions are done in love, as a guide.

They are able to dig into the guts and take on tough issues and sensitive to see what is subtly happening. They can do this because they make wise decisions by *recognizing subtle*

77

differences or indicators that others do not. They are able to take calculated risks, like delegate certain tasks to others to do their will, because they have learned from experience when to take such risk based on odds of success and trust.

In a nutshell, they are able to both think and feel outside-the-box in the face of battle or circumstances,

To master a new form of communication, you must develop the ability to rapidly learn techniques and master the right tools and questions.

- Learn to adapt to change by answering correctly the questions raised by changed conditions. How many forces do we need? Mission

Command, Critical Events, Risks, Money needed, Legal (Authorities and Agreements) , Key Leader Engagements (KLEs) or Facilities and Forces, Access, Basing, and Influence (F^2AB-I).

- Combine historical identifiable trends in leadership and manpower quality as a point to start your analysis.
- Know about the struggle between the warrior and manager mentality - Efficiency versus Effectiveness debate.

Nevertheless, when Generals guess wrong, they are adaptable and roll up their sleeves and do the tasks themselves, because they can rely on their savviness, if need be to outmaneuver and move around obstacles. They know the rules and when to bend them and break them. Artists like, Mozart, Newton, and Socrates are prime examples. As well as, Beethoven, Goethe, and Hemingway.

When it comes time to stay on issues, change gears and switch up actions, they are not afraid and you can count on them. They sometime pull strings that only they know how to pull.

Third, they know the equipment or tools that are central to each pillar or organization and how they were designed to work together to produce a certain result. Knowing the capabilities or specifications of equipment and tools allows them to understand how much they can do and help determine when outside help might be needed. They have keen insight into processes as well and how processes can be leveraged or mixed to build the greatest capacity to respond to ever-changing environments. They know how to work a system by recruiting and building teams, coalitions, networks, and clusters of the well-connected that support each other.

The key to their success is their empathetic ability to ask the relevant and important questions within each pillar of power. This ability allows them to *play the game* well and get the deal done by determining the worth, authorities, and rewards associated with each pillar of power.

As you read this book, think about what a person of power does and says and you repeat it and know that you to have what they have; impact, influence, an ability to effect change by calling the shots, and a willingness to stand firm when they see wrong.

The experience gained from taking a center of gravity approach allows you to obtain confidence in your decisions and what you believe you are seeing. Most people only believe what they can see. **It is those who can see what they believe in and understand the processes that supports it before it becomes a reality are those that become really successful in life.** It allows you to establish a central point of view to clearly see the lines of thought /thinking that support events. It also lets you see the many sides or vantage points that are on the extremes of that line of thought/thinking that reaches out to the *width and depth of points of view.*

You can then use the strategies to see the many sides of issues. Sometimes the ideal solution will not equate to the optimal solution with respect to the overall plan. You will be able to see, infer, connect, and then make rapid conclusions about the issues before you that are relevant to your life.

What are the indications, impressions, suggestions, questions, symbols, imagery, or answers that you are getting from what you are now seeing, feeling, and hearing?

Next, what can you infer from what you see? Where in the news have you seen this or heard this before from experience or knowing? What do you already know about the information or have learned? What do you need to re-look about what you know?

You must know where to look and what to look for. You are looking for patterns so that you can make connections that allow you to see some degree of harmony or order over the short term, mid-term, and long term.

The next thing you want to do is connect with the information. What new things does it make you think about? What does it make you want to do, say, see, or write about? What human, things, plants, animals can best illustrate the new information that you are thinking about? *Use your imagination* and your five senses to connect the information gained from the news.

Finally, you want to conclude on the basis of having an understanding of the new information and integrating it within your decision-making process to determine the best course of action concerning the new insight.

What you need to do is elevate your critical thinking skills and be able to adjust your actions while you are in constant motion. You must determine your center of gravity for processes and organizations and be aware of when you are crossing an important decision point or in a decisive moment. You have to ask yourself:

What is the fixed base(s) of operations? What is the main objective point? Where is the forward line of troops, strategic fronts, and line of defense? What are your zones of and lines of operations? Where are your temporary strategic lines of communications? Where are your natural and man-made obstacles? Where are your geographic strategic points that you might need to occupy? Where are your intermediate bases of operations? What is the strategic value of each location's capability?

What are the strategic geometric directions you are seeing from this new understanding? What is the overall flow or movement of products/services? Is the movement increasing or decreasing? What position do you hold in the market? When does that position reach peak production or distribution? Are the key rates rising or declining? What trends are you seeing? Is cost increasing or decreasing? What specific movements can you detect in the distribution of products and services? What relationships do you need to establish or relationships that need to be changed? Finally, what distribution processes and organizations are moving in the right direction and those that are not and need to change?

For example, in thinking, focused on distribution-based logistics, you will need to know the rules of thumb, guidelines or metrics you will use to get a sense of whether you are on track to achieve your expectations. You must be able to see what products and services you have purchased, what's in inventory, what is being maintained, what has been ordered and is in transit to you. You have to monitor how fast and what is the time that you will definitely have the product or service on-hand.   From this sequence of data points, you will need to identify redundancies by integrating, enhancing, seeing, and synchronizing your planning and operating processes against buffers that will allow you to cover consumption and replenishment cycles, preventing distribution disruptions. These buffers are based on risk tolerance that mitigate risk without creating waste and overburdening the transportation system.

Exponential Distribution and Sensing of Sharper Layers as FORCE FIELD WIZARDRY

Wisdom will be developed by instinctively judging what right action to take, based on knowledge, insight, experience, common sense, and understanding to see things differently, more broadly, and deeply.

Here's another good example of practical application of the thought processes discussed in this book. Now, National Military Strategy is built upon three pillars of being able to respond, able to shape, and able to prepare for future operations and emerging trends.

Generals are able to perform their missions that support all three of these pillars within distributed networks. These networks consist of four types: **Physical (concerned with Quantity, Capacity), Financial (concerned with the movement of money), Informational (concerned with systems data collection), and Communications** (concerned with linkage of systems/processes).

National Power is based upon Strategic Geometry of four pillars: political and diplomatic, economic, informational/technological, and military. By using each pillar, one can defeat obstacles whether they are on strategic, operational, or tactical in scope.

Generals use FORCE FIELD WIZARDRY to link strategic design to tactics or objective to events. They do this by sequencing of objectives and events over time, space, and function. They instinctively know when they go beyond their culmination point and adjust

resources to compensate as they
extend their operational reach.

Time, space, and function mean looking at
decision points, lines of communications,
culminating points, indirect approaches,
positional advantages and strategic
concentration of resources, and deception.
Generals use triangulation of Land, Sea,
Air, Space, Cyberspace in support of
operations using a layered/relational
networked geometry/spatial projection of
forces and fluid flow distribution that
allows exponential growth in flexibility,
precision, and coordination to adapt to any
environment.

They look for advantages and things that
allow greater initiatives.

Decision points add significant advantages. They are the most critical points and objectives that allow the greatest flexibility and momentum. They are key to defeating or protecting a center of gravity. Usually, there are more decision points than there are resources to cover them. Decision points are usually geographic, such as a sea-lane, a town, airfield, or boundaries, airspace. They indicate a point at which one must determine the best use of available resources and weigh that use against risk.

Lines of communication defines the direction of resources to the obstacles and objectives. They connect your resources from your base of operations to where the resources are needed on the ground. In the future, you can expect the lines of communication to be supported over extended distances by disbursed small units.

Culminating point is that point when you overextend your resources and can no longer sufficiently continue the momentum. Generals keep an eye on that fact that distance decreases capacity and efficiencies past this point.

The indirect approach allows you to move from unexpected directions or times.

Generals are masters of *operational art and design*. The know how to achieve objectives by sequencing of operations and use of resources in phases, branches and sequels, sequential and simultaneous warfare,

93

and precision logistics that is reliable, responsive, and agile.

Sequencing of operations is *the visualization* of what it takes to achieve the end result. You sequence objectives, decision points, culmination points, and priorities over time and space. You look at centers of gravity and culminating points to envision requirements for each branch or sequel. Sequencing is useful when determining phases of operations. Each phase of operations should lay the groundwork for future efforts. All tasks to be accomplished under each phase and why it is important for that task to be accomplished under a specific phase should be addressed.

Generals also visualize how requirements will be filled by branches or contingency plans use of resources. Visualization allows the Generals the ability to do the parallel planning and provides them more of a valuable resource – **time and speed**.

They are able to ask and find the answers to what is relevant and what is the meaning or implication of what I'm seeing? What is the optimal? Minimal requirement? What is the probability of this or that happening? What are the acceptable risks and the tensions that I am see because of that risk? Who else needs to know this information and should be involved in the decision-making? Who should be sitting at the table?

You need to be able to focus those key people by identifying tasks and subtasks, determining what is important and at what risk, and asking how can you facilitate the process?

Now, what you should not do is lose sight of the big picture, look only at short-term actions, or assume that you can use a fixed way to solve distribution management problems.

Generals use the Central Position and Indicator Thinking.

They gain a holistic understanding that they are part of a much larger, more complex supply chain with the goal of reduction or shrinking of time-distance between strategic geometry and lines of communication forces.

They make sense of the global environment: Making sense means knowing supply and movement rates at different <u>levels</u> of the logistics enterprise and how to mitigate actions based upon known and unforeseen requirements. These efforts allow for the reduction or shrinking of time-distance between strategic geometry and lines of communication forces.

They understand and ask, what is the current distribution system in place based on? They also attempt to define the system:

Definition of Battlefield Distribution System = what are the keywords that are the interaction or the quality of the interaction between Processes, Capabilities, and End Users.

Key components needed to understand the system are:

1 - Asset Visibility (What can I see in real-time?)

2 - Environmental Factors (What may influence actions/decisions?)

3 - Prediction of Future Capability to Move Items (Forecasting Requirements based on indicators)

The process starts with the End-User, next the process for tracking assets: for example, in the Army, Global Combat Support System – Army (GCCS-A) Inventory Activities, next what capability is required to store supplies, what material handling equipment (MHE) is needed, and finally what transportation is required to move the supplies. All three components have their own internal and external environmental factors that contribute to delay within the system. These factors must be identified and understood by all within the system to achieve efficiency and effectiveness of the system.

By having visibility and an upgrade in truck technology/capabilities, MHE, and Radio Frequency Identification (RFID), one will be able to re-route items/trucks while on the move based on priorities/unanticipated events.

One could also use the latest Global Distribution Management Systems to assist with asset visibility.

Still one must look at the Environment (It consists of conditions, circumstances, and influences).

In the military, we look at the Political, Military, Economic, Social, Intellectual, and Technological elements. Key here is to determine priorities based upon supply and movement rates and communicating this so leaders can determine mitigation actions and still achieve success at some acceptable risk.

Acceptable risk must be assumed in three of the following areas:

  - Process – Command and Control, Reporting, Asset Visibility

  - Capability - Facilities and equipment needed to receive, store, move materials

  - End Users - generate requirements and indicators of their need

One must look at the links between internal and external relationships accounting for different information requirements at different levels over time...looking for similar rates/patterns that are revealed and seen as FORCE FIELD WIZARDRY, delays, or after-action assessments.

Four-Step Process:

Key to understanding the Central Position and Indicator Thinking is a four-step process:

1. Identify and focus on the critical/most important tasks to success.

2. Explain why critical tasks are priority over other tasks.

3. Focus on decisions needed to make over phases.

4. Explain what conditions would exist at the end of each phase and at end-state. Backward plan on needs to achieve objectives by seeing the triggers and indicators that shows significant change to decision points.

The areas that do not change when planning in any environments are:

1. Location
2. Decision Points
3. Defense/Protection
4. Offense/Attack
5. Where can I apply Speed
6. Where can I apply Surprise/Deception

Remember this because it is key:

The driving issue/criteria is how much **RISK** are you willing to accept? That is…Acceptable Risk. Examples of criteria are your ability to **SEE** things, **PRESSURES** on key lines of communications, **DAMAGE** to infrastructure, etc.

Examples of triggers and indicators are those things that **SIGNIFICANTLY** change or affect mission outcome; adjustments to guidance, definitions, environmental, and approaches, and of course, adjustments to timing.

More than ever, you must seek next level simplification - simplification in technology, distribution management, and in driving efficient order out of chaos.

Simplicity starts with powerful yet flexible knowledge that makes it faster and easier for you to see real time solutions to problems. You will focus on the distribution systems rates and levels that increases efficiencies and thus reduce delays and increases customer satisfaction.

In a world where thinking and technology are growing exponentially, the wrong distribution system bogging down by delays means your problems aren't being efficiently solved. Reliability, response time, and scalability matter. Time is money— slow response times mean less customer satisfaction and efficiency. With 100% visibility and the fastest response times in your industry, you maximize your time-delivery. Plus, you get real-time updates with no delay.

Indicator Thinking provides complete visibility into your logistics data, allowing you to monitor performance, act on insights and drive effective distribution strategies.

Key Features of the Central Position and FORCE FIELD WIZARDRY Include:

Sense of Operational Design: a three-area platform that empowers you determine how far you can go, how fast you need to move within, and how long you need to sustain your distribution system to optimize performance. The key areas are operational reach/depth (determines how far you need go), operational tempo/rate (determines how fast), and Operational Sustainment

/Direction (determines how long you need to stay in a location and sustain supply and distribution systems). All three elements provide the planner with the sense of the operational design.

Framework Design: Uncover rich, powerful guiding principles, goals, and conceptual underpinnings that deliver business-critical insight in seconds. Potential inputs to guiding principles could be CEO directives and who does he need to influence to move the company to success. Goals can be made by taking time to visualize what ends the CEO wants. Conceptual underpinnings that must be address in any planning effort would be the number of people needed, equipment readiness rates, any training or specialized training needed, and to determine what relationships must be established.

Leader Input: Identify the CEO's intent, see gaps created by war-gaming to identify true requirements and the roles and expectations that support the CEO's intent. Get what the CEO's vision is. As you continue planning, you will come to a point where you will war-game or determine the requirements and gaps identified in the planning effort. What are roles and expectations he sees? Who is going to do what?

Insights: Dashboard that provides holistic performance insights to track, drill, measure and links to crucial business metrics. Insights allow you to create multiple distribution ideas. You will gain insights into strategic direction, overall and specific changes to make, key positioning status, trends, distribution, requirement, readiness, technology, and relationship changes. Insights provide a sense of whether these areas are increasing or decreasing. You can get a general feel based upon either subjective measures or objective measures/metrics like the number of equipment on-hand or with no maintenance problems. Another example would be the trends in spending, resources used, and distribution hubs increasing or decreasing.

Rules of Thumb: Dashboard that provides general/standardized performance measures to track, drilldown, and act on crucial business metrics for your industry. Metrics on how long (time-distance) it will take to move supplies and equipment by air, seas, and land or the time it will take to contract the supplies and equipment or services. If you chose to obtain the supplies, equipment, or services from other countries, what is the Customs access time in days? What are rules of thumb when determining force requirements?

In logistics, here are some Rules of Thumb to remember:

When planning a theater opening package, build and sequence your TPFDD by starting with the Mission Command Structure that is needed to command and control the sustainment environment. Normally, a Sustainment Brigade supported by a Combat Sustainment Support Battalion (CSSB) will be enough to do the job, although that can be modified to meet mission requirements. The Sustainment

Brigade and CSSB can influence the battlefield from minutes, hours, days, to weeks. Other logistics enablers like the Expeditionary Sustainment Command and Theater Sustainment Command can influence the battlefield from weeks to months. The CSSB has an organic headquarters and headquarters company and are task organized with composite and functional sustainment companies, teams, and detachments. A typical, a task organized CSSB has six functional capabilities, a composite supply company, support maintenance company, modular ammunition company, palletized load system truck company, and inland cargo transfer company, and a field feeding company. The CSSB operates the class I (subsistence) and water warehouse, supply support activity (SSA), class III (bulk petroleum) fuel farm, forward arming and refueling point, retail fuel point, ammunition supply point, and central receiving and shipping point (CRSP). This CSSB can be outfitted with whole units or composite teams called Forward Logistics Elements (FLE) that are tailored to meet the mission requirements for a Multi-Modal operation. Next you would look at the logistics functional areas that a FLE would execute and determine the number of people it would take to support the mission. A typical FLE can consist of between 9 – 45 people, with an average size of 20 people. It will generally be composed of the following functional areas:

FLE OIC/NCOIC (2 people)

Composite Supply Platoon:

CL I (Food) (2 people), CL I (Water) (1-3 people) (Field Feeding Teams)

CL III Coordinator (1 person)
(Medium Truck Platoon
w/maintenance)

CL III (Fuel) (2-4 people)

CL V (Munitions) (1-3 people)
(Ordnance Support Maintenance
Company)

Movement Control Team
(Transportation) (2-5 people) (Heavy
Equipment Transfer Platoon
w/maintenance

Passenger Movement (2 people)

Maintenance Support Teams (CL IX
parts requisitioned through GCSS-A
(1-4 people) (Support Maintenance
Platoon)

SAMs Clerk (1 person) (Human
Resource/Postal/Gateway)

Finance Clerk (1 person)

Postal Clerk (1-2 people)

Medical (Area Support) (1-5 people)

Signal Clerks (3 people)

Mortuary Affairs (1 person)

Contractors/LOGCAP Team (as needed)

These would establish a logistics hub to manage things like Fuel points, Ammunition Supply Points, Supply Support Activity, and Retrograde Property Assistance Team (RPAT) yards.

Other logistics Rules of Thumbs:

- When establishing a supply support base, make sure you have 2-3 access points to be able to resupply the base.

- Rail and Ship is best for large movement of equipment.

- A double-line railroad, under wartime conditions, can move at least 50 or more trains (400 tons each) a day or

20K tons a day. A Two- lane road can do it at greater expense.

- A non-mechanized army requires only 15-30 pounds of supply per man per day. Every 1K tons of supply keeps 100K men in combat for a day. Even if supply below those levels, combat capability won't be reduced until over 33% of the requirement is denied. After that point 1 percent of the combat power is lost. Most units retain 33% of its combat power.

- Mechanized units require over 10 times as much supply per man. (Fuel key here 60% of movement, Ammunition 20% movement).

- Two places where logistics is key; wilderness (deserts, jungles, mountains, etc.) and small islands.

Still one must look at the Environment (It consists of conditions, circumstances, and influences).

Key Inputs: See levels of priority, domain, threat, power, and their significance and weights. The three levels that you will work with are on a strategic, operational, or tactical level. You will be trying to determine when a shift on one level impacts or shifts actions on another level. Domains are on a physical level, Cognitive level, or Moral level (Is it ethical?) What are threats? Are they a local, regional, or global threat? What impacts the elements of National Power – Political, Military, Economic, Social, Intellectual, and Influence? What are the impacts of unknown or unanticipated inputs?

Risk Development: Two elements that should always be in the back of your mind when making decisions about acceptable risk: What is the risk to your mission and risk to people? Risks to mission can be major changes to lines of communications, lead-times for obtaining resources, available inventories on hand, or actions that increase or decrease requirements. Mal-positioned resources could also impact risk to mission. Risk to people could be the number of people available and their skillset. You can also look at ratios to determine if you have a good harmony in your capability versus a competitor. In the military, if one is on the defense, one would want a 1:3 ratio in operations to obtain success. If on the offense, one would want a 3:1 ratio. The next level to risk development is to determine when risk to mission shifts or exceeds the risk to force and then determine the mitigation strategies/actions that must be applied to achieve your desired effects/results.

Metrics: Identifies the key criteria when developing business metrics – determining when an action is efficient (uses the least number of steps) and effective (It works, regardless of steps/costs). Some Key Performance Indicators (KPI) are estimate of probability, relative or optimal value, trade-offs in time-cost, benefits, risks and opportunities, tensions and when are they in balance, price to cost, what are the significance, implications, and consequences, what is the priorities for essential information. To me one of the most critical metrics are what are the supply and movement rates.

Mitigation Strategies: Optional strategies you can use in scenario planning, course of action development, and war-gaming. Use scenario planning to look at the ideal scenario and what you would like to have happen, likely to happen or is more realistic, and then what could happen, but not likely to happen. Do you need to expand lines of communications, forecast requirements, preposition people and materials, prioritize and establish supply rates for supplies, establish manning levels, expand contracts, solicit support from other partners, and establish agreements that will allow for quicker and better understanding of operational requirements in determining when authorities /agreements are needed and how they will be used.

Key Outputs: Expected business effects/outputs that are the result of Business Intelligence Insights that lead to modified plans and planning. Other key outputs would be a good list of mission command size, how much money is needed, legal issues resolved, risks mitigated, and critical events determined. One could also look at capability at each location, impact, and why the capability is needed at that location. Still other key outputs could be that the main effort required is weighted, knowledge of the culminating point and line of diminishing returns, and knowledge of choke points and a validated synchronization of logistics in support of operations. Desired effects/outputs must be determined based on capabilities. Based upon the desired effects/outputs, you must identify priorities given the effects/outputs. You can also determine what do you maximize or minimize/highlight or hide. These outputs impact your reporting.

Reporting: Map visualizations maximize the ability to recognize the most important drivers that deliver efficient and effective outcomes. Standard reporting delivers the insight necessary to track metrics of performance and drive efficient and effective decision-making. You can report on the background (why you are taking action), Assessment (Who, What, and How and action is executed), and the Way Ahead (When, with time horizons 5 years, 1 year, Quarterly, Monthly, Weekly, and Daily). You first **THINK** about what you expect to see, hear, and learn, **SEE**

the current operating environment, **THINK** about what you have seen, heard, or learned, and then **DO**, take actions on what you now see, hear, and learn. This is the **THINK-SEE-THINK- DO** cycle. You can then summarize a complex problem in a few pithy sentences and report information that allows you to focus and act on the prioritized data that matters from most important to least, least controversial to most, negative to positive (always end on positive note), and then provide your recommendations and thoughts about multiple delivery options ensure you receive the insights needed to maximize strategic, operational, and tactical efficiencies. You will be able to unlock new insights to other critical areas of your business that will allow you to better understand and make sense of key drivers, themes, and talking points that influence each other to achieve the best outcome.

Planning Mastery

SENSE OF OPERATIONAL...
* REACH/DEPTH (FAR)
* TEMPO/RATE (FAST)
* SUSTAINMENT/DIRECTION/LONG)

FRAMEWORK:
* GUIDING PRINCIPLE (Influence/Cmd Directives)
* GOAL (Endstate)
* CONCEPTUAL UNDERPINNINGS (People/Readiness/Tng/Relations)

LEADER INPUT
* CDR'S INTENT (Vision)
* WARGAMING (GAPS) (Assign Roles/Solve for Results)
* Requirements (Wargaming)
* Roles (Cdr's Intent)
* Expectations (Cdr's Intent)

INSIGHTS

* STRATEGIC DIRECTION
* OVERALL/SPECIFIC RELOCATION +/-
* POSITIONING - Posture/Peak
* TRENDS - S, Habits, Resources
* TECHNOLOGY

* DISTRIBUTION +/-
* REQUIREMENTS - Increasing/Decreasing
* READINESS
* RELATIONSHIPS - To Establish/Change

"Every Force Has Its Counter Motion"

RULES OF THUMB
* 150 Miles from FLOT
* 90 Miles / Day
* Air = (15/5 Days)
* Ground = 14 Days)
* Sea =30 Days
* Contracts 12-30, 30-60, 71-90+Days
* Customs Access - 25 Days
* FLE (Range 10 - 45+ pax)

RISK
* MSN : (+/- LOCs, Lead-Times, Available Inventories, Actions that +/- Requirements)
* Mal-positioned Resources
* FORCE: (#s/Ratios, Skillset)

KEY INPUTS
* PRIORITIES (Strategic/Opnl/ Tactical Shifts)
* DOMAIN (Physical, Cognitive, Moral)
* THREAT (Local, Region, Global)
* PMESII
* SIGNIFICANCE/WEIGHT
* UNKNOWNS

METRICS
* Estimate of Probability
* Relative Value/Optimal
* Trade-offs (Time/Cost)
* Risk/Opportunity
* Tensions(When Balance Achieved)
* Price/Cost
* Rates (Supply + Mvt Factors)
* Significance
* Implications/Consequences
* Priorities (Essential Information)

* EFFICIENT (Least number of Steps)

* EFFECTIVE (It Works)

KEY OUTPUTS
* L x V x C x W = V2
* MC, $, Legal, Risks, Critical Events
* F2AB-I
* Weight ME
* Culminating Point
* Line of Diminishing Returns
* Sufficiency of LOCs
* Maintenance Priorities
* Logistics Synchronization
* Assessments
* Identify Choke Points
* Border Access
* APODS/SPODs
* Modified Plans

MITIGATION
* Expand LOCs
* Forecasting Requirements
* Prepo Staff/Materials
* Prioritize/Establish CSRs
* Capacity Analysis
* FML Established
* Expand Contracts
* Partners (HNS)
* Agreements

REPORTING
* BACKGROUND (Why)
* ASSESSMENT (Who, What, How)
* WAY AHEAD w/PLANNING (When) HORIZONS (5-1-QMWD)
* SUMMARIZE:
  - Most important to Least
  - Least Controversial to Most
  - Negative to Positive
  - Recommendation
  - Your Thoughts

Dr. Joseph Graham

Figure 1 Planning Mastery Matrix

Controlled Simplicity

Control

Giving back control to customers is our top priority. You gain control when your solutions provide the flexibility and agility to meet your unique business needs. By combining your expertise and our user-friendly thinking model, you achieve new levels of controlling striated space for efficiency.

Simplicity

More than ever, customers seek next level simplification - simplification in technology, distribution management, and in driving efficient order out of chaos. Simplicity starts with powerful yet flexible knowledge that makes it faster and easier for you to see real time solutions to problems. You will focus on the distribution systems rates and levels that increases efficiencies and thus reduce delays and increases customer satisfaction. Simplicity allows you to see when an operating environment shifts. These shifts are tied to information priorities that have been determined by the CEO or leadership as they look for indicators, pressures, triggers, decision points, and develop timelines.

For example, what's critical to sustainment in general and distribution management specifically is first to identify your major sustainment hubs and lines of communications (LOCs) and determining whether they are mature or not, then looking at supporting LOCs and seeing when there is a shift from the major LOCs to the supporting LOCs being the major hub. This happens when the supporting LOCs have built up Days of Supply (DOS) of commodities and supplies forward. Important in this determination is the that you have continuity of resources, which is that you have the number of required commodities, that can be tracked by a Distribution Boards that looks at schedules and movement times, sustainment support platforms and required force protection IOT balance maintenance, sustainment cycles, and driver rest cycles. This give the process continuity and certainty, taking into account cycle adjustments and intra and inter-area support operations. Finally, you have to take advantage of automation tools/enablers that will allow you to see the battlefield/environment. Seeing the environment makes the logistical situation predictable because of situational awareness. From this process, you can determine if the distribution network is mature which means it slows down the operational tempo and allows for more time to analyze and assess the logistical posture. A mature distribution network over time improves the logistical posture and expands the decision space.

The Center of Gravity within a logistics framework is the number of Distribution Boards that are required to manage the logistical reporting and sustainment cycle and planning timelines. Units that are forward request requirements and send the request for commodities and resources backward to be filled as resources arrive in theater within a proper timeline so they can be received, stored, onward moved, and integrated (RSOI for supplies) to sustain combat operations forward.

Units use logistical reporting that consists up to a 72+ hour sustainment cycle and 180+ hours planning timeline for theater sustainment units to send supplies to forward units IOT sustain combat operations. The 72 -180 hours timeline is the COG or sweet spot that is critical to successful logistical operations.

Now, I've been retired from the military since 2008 and have had time to meditate on my 20-year experiences and will share my insight gained during peacetime and wartime on decision-making and how the Generals I knew thought that can be applied to FORCE FIELD WIZARDRY.

Before I get to that, I want to share with you some coincidences that I found to be interesting about my life. The path that I have taken seemed familiar to me. Like I'd been there and done that before. I find coincidences, in places, in particularly interesting.

I've always had a connection with, it seems, General William T. Sherman, of the Union Army. It seemed like I rode with him on his campaign through the South and my current military assignments lined-up with the places he marched. It's like I could see eye to eye with him and had a sense of having known him always; in essence on the same path, road, truths, experiencing the beauties, errors, stars of life. One day, I sat back and thought, "this is weird".

General Sherman marched through Atlanta, Savannah, GA, and burned Columbia, SC. I was stationed in all three cities and now live in Columbia, SC. I was born 1964, one hundred years after General Sherman marched through Atlanta in 1864. There seems to be a connection with 100 years rebirth in reincarnation circles/beliefs. Not only that, my relatives on my mother's side last name is Sherman; although my relatives on my father's side last name is Davis. The first crush I had on girl had the last name of Lee. So being around Generals seemed normal to me because it seemed to be in my DNA.

So being around the select group of people who have "real power" who are the "go to" individuals who make it

things happen seem to be normal.
Again, I witnessed this during my
military career, when the U.S. Army
would bring in a select group of people,
usually Generals, to manage a military
campaign. You could call them the
"Dream Team". This Dream Team is in
all successful organizations and must be
searched out when you encounter each
pillar that supports the Power Hub
discussed in earlier chapters of this
book.

Prior to and during the Iraq War, I had the
opportunity to brief and sit in a room of
Generals to discuss plans. The things that I
noticed about how they make decisions are
amazing. They are indeed rare individuals,
with each having a singularity of focus
based on their background experiences.

Traits that I noted about them, they were an uncommon group that displayed imagination, instinct, calm, speaking ability, charismatic, with physical size, and daring in their attitude. They had an almost poetic or rhythmic way of thinking.

Each had an organizational mind and just seemed brilliant in determining how to get results from chaos by having a process to *filter incoming information.*

Over my career, I've been blessed to work with and shook hands with brilliant Generals with names such as Christianson, Shelton, Thurmond, Franks, Wallace, Jones, and many others. Their unique ability and art at asking questions of others and evaluate the response were the key underpinnings to their strength. They also had a birds-eye view of organizational structures, systems, and processes and how they work on different levels to achieve strategic, operational, and tactical success.

They could see current disposition and anticipate future needs in an ever-flowing risky environment. They did this by looking for impressions, indicators, and deploying sensors within the environment to see the power within it to address top-tier problems even in an asymmetric environment.

To have power or the ability to influence and control things to get things done, you must know what power is, it's pillars of support and the functions within each, such as the people who work there and their certifications/training levels, their reach or influence, the equipment or tools that they use, the systems they put together to produce output, and the processes used to make the system work. You should focus on the costs, savings, and efficiencies gained.

Now here is the key to opening the door to understanding life by using what I call Exponential Thinking applied to obstacles that you face in your life to filter incoming information from all sources like the Generals did.

Discovering the truth, the secret to understanding Exponential Thinking is this:

The ability to think and act faster than the competition using sensors and sharper networks.

To understand exponentially increasing information, you must decrease your thinking by assigning color codes to what the information means to you, and then determine the centers of gravity of the codes from your known position or point, or what I sometimes call; your X spot.

X is everywhere apparent, but nowhere stated directly.

You have often seen X and heard of X when you were shown a treasure map with a dotted line and arrow that lead to a spot on the map that had the X on it.

Most of us, say that the X is where the treasure is buried.

We often overlook the X; while focusing on the buried treasure. We even say "X marks the spot".

The X is the secret of secrets. Knowing X determines the worth, authorities, and rewards that lead to strategic geometry and wisdom.

You have seen a football game, and when someone wants to show how a play develops, they use X's and O's. We pay attention to the X's and O's, but don't see the secret, which is being shown right before us.

In mathematics, we say, "solve for X".
Now, X is the secret to understanding
Exponential Thinking that will allow you to
understand what to do with the
 an ever-increasing amount of news and
information that is coming at you.

X stands for the Roman number ten. In
numbers, it is represented as 10.
Our numbering system is based on ten.

Computers communicate using 1 and 0.

They use a binary code of 10^7, 10^6, 10^5, 10^4,
10^3, 10^2, 10^1, 10^0. So you get 10^1 x 1 = 10,
10^2 = 100, 10^3 = 1,000, and so forth.

For every sequence, you get 10 times the
result.

It gets away from the linear way we think and provides information 10 times for every sequence or count.

To keep up with the information coming at you, we've discovered that you must use the following three sequences:

Sequence 1: Reduce information coming at you to its *root or basic name*. Further, reduce the basic name using substrings. For example, prosperity, has a root name of prospering, a substring to that would be *pro* and *sper*. You can then add a pre-fix or suffix to the word to extend or create additional word meanings like prosper*ed,* prosper*ing, etc.* Adding -ed, -er, -ing, -ly allows you to expand into greater meaning/ language.

Using substrings allow you to reduce the information down to its sub-elements. At the substring level, you can begin to attach meaning to words like an incomplete puzzle. You simply begin to see each letter as an indicator of the word, sentence, or paragraph that is about to come.

It is also at this level that you will start to attach a value to what the letter, words "is" and what it "does". Is it relevant to what you are imagining or desiring?

Once you get its meaning, you move on to sequence 2.

Sequence 2: You assign a color to the word. The color represents whether the word represents a threat or friendly results for you. If you perceive the word as a threat, you use the color red. If you perceive it as friendly, you use green. If you perceive it as neutral, use yellow.

Assigning a color to words, allows you to see threats quicker. As you know, one of the first things the eye notices when walking into a room is color. It then tries to determine the shape, so the next tool you can use it the element of line/shape. Your eye will try to determine the pattern if one is discernible.

Now colors can be of a Hue, Intensity, or Value. This can be shown if the color is determined to be a hot or cold, warm or cool, color. This can be shown by different shades or tints.

The line element can be shown as horizontal, vertical, diagonal, or curvilinear. Typically, Horizontal reveals width and side-to-side movement, vertical lines reveal height or up and down movement, diagonal reveals angle or dynamic interest, and curvilinear reveals tension.

Being able to see the line or shape and color will allow you to determine whether what you are seeing is friendly or not.

What you are looking for is what in graphic design we call harmony or balance. You are looking for a fluid flow of thought.

When you see something in balance, it means that you have the capability to meet whatever information is coming at you. If you see something that is out of balance and is represented by the color "red" then, you know that you will automatically pay attention to it because it is not friendly. Look for the little details that are so critical to the support of greater things.

You would then use the line element to determine if it is heading directly at you or from an angle.

All of this takes place in seconds or less and leads to the Sharper Thinking.

What you are doing is using the nature or built in the way your body is designed to recognize things. It is one of the driving factors that has to allow humans to continue to exist, the survival instinct.

Plus, you are using what you desire and your ability to be curious about things or your curiosity to imagine what information is coming at you. (strategic foresight)

These factors determine your perception of what you see or make suggestions of what might be in the near future.

Finally, Sequence 3: Use Center of Gravity concepts to place the colors on a *mental map*.

Take the colors and picture them in your mind as if they are on a map. You will put yourself in the spot shown in the center of the X.

There must be a move to develop your thinking using the concept of center of gravity. You have to determine your decision points and vulnerabilities in order to solve the current problems and protect yourself from a large amount of information that is being generated. Again, Claude Von Clausewitz felt that center of gravity is the concentration of "hub" of power. From that point or position, place all of the "red" colors, then the "yellow" colors, and finally, the "green" colors.

This will reveal to you the threats that the incoming information may have on you.

Use your curiosity or imagination at this time to allow you to read and judge the focal point and how colors/things are categorized or grouped around the point.

It will allow you to ask if there is a natural balance of resources? What is the weight of the various components and will the foundations support them?

You can use these three sequences for they are the secret master key to exponential thinking. This process will allow you to see things coming sooner and give you some reaction time that others who are not using this process will not have.

It is the seed to your success.

In every word is the seed to its mastery. Information has within it the seeds of success. We just have to use this substring, color-coded, and center of gravity process to reach success.

Now that you know what the X is, you must start using it today. You have taken the road less traveled.

That road is to be consciously taken until it becomes an unconscious habit **(e^t)** or double exponential thinking.
This must be done daily.

What you see reflected will then create in you the feelings and skills that you need and desire to become a more confident person.

It is not an easy road to follow, because most people naturally don't do it.

FLOW 4

It has been widely accepted that you must develop your mind to be able to think far and wide, expanding your mind, while reaching into the big wide world in any event. You may do that by doing or imagining how to explore the broad view/context with intuitive judgment.

Think deeply and wide about your experiences and how these experiences will shape your world in general.

It is the conceptual phase that requires creativity, intelligence, thought, and an understanding of the many subtle influences (calculus) bearing on problems. Strategic thinkers with broad view of planning will be needed to develop outlook and judgment into a comprehensive and integrated plan.

LOGISTICS FLOW is a 3-by-3 comprehensive and integrated three category, nine-step thinking process that you can use to solve more problems and make better decisions by collaboration and asking essential questions.

What I've discovered is that there is a rhythm to logistics planning, a flow, that must be synchronized with the operational rhythm. Both must harmonize using the principle of center of gravity within the contextual framework. This logistics rhythm must remain visible in the mind of the thinker/planner from the moment supplies move through the distribution system. You've got to have checkpoints within the distribution system so you can have some control of the system. You can use these checkpoints to see supplies as they move from entering a theater at an airfield, to the theater distribution center, transportation cargo transfer location, and ultimately to the user. At each of these points, you need to establish performance metrics to see how well the system is doing. But most of all, there the distribution system must be owned by one entity, for example a Logistics Operations Center that is perhaps supported by a Transportation Operation Center.

LOGISTICS FLOW Reversed

Category 1: MIC

- Step 1 - M: METT-TC
- Step 2 - I: Influences
- Step 3 - C: Capability

Category 2: A^3

- Step 4 - A: Approach
- Step 5 - A^2: Assumptions
- Step 6 - A^3: Action

Category 3: BLT

- Step 7 - B: Broad Concept
- Step 8 - L: Logistics
- Step 9 - T: Total Analysis and Assessment

Category 1: MIC

Step 1: METT-TC is a (US, military, mnemonic) Initials of mission, enemy, terrain, troops available, time, and civilian considerations. It is used by the United States military to help commanders remember the considerations in the planning of any operation. When using METT-TC, it allows you to determine what is required. You will first look at the Enemy's Center of Gravity (ECOG) in people, equipment, maintenance, etc., Friendly Non-Linear Center of Gravity (FNLCOG), the capability of both enemy and friendly forces, and then the standards that you want to achieve and adhere to.

1. Can the specific operations necessary to accomplish the objective, can or cannot be determined at this time? (METT-TC)
2. Given the nature and scope of operations, what must you do to satisfy the will to win?
3. What is necessary to develop? Forces, flexibility? (FNLCoG)
4. What is the estimated EN capability with standards of what they can do? (ECoG)

Step 2: Influences is where you look at the lines of communications; air, ground, sea, space, and cyber that you have want to achieve a degree of success.

1. State/List the important influences – i.e. air superiority, sea, ground LOCs, SECFOR
2. State the degree of success given effectiveness and timeliness
3. List any assumptions leading to success

Step 3: Capability is where you determine equipment and mobilization capabilities required.

1. List any imperatives to production/ that must be produced.
2. Appropriate distribution of forces?
3. What type force is needed TF, Conventional?
4. Partner Nation and Home Nation force capability?

Category 2: A^3

Step 4: Approach is where you determine the type of approach required. Here you will use the 5 W's as discussed earlier in this book. Priority of the 5 W's will be **How** you plan to accomplish things, **When** you plan to accomplish things, and then the other acronyms.

1. Approach to achieving means using 5W's.

153

2. Where? (Location)
3. How? (US and PN/HN forces
4. Key areas to control? (sea, air, enemy economic and industrial life, LOCs, raw materials)
5. Show where enemies are over-extended, dispersed, shortage of resources happen, will lost.

Step 5: Assumption is where you question the assumptions that you are using as a basis of employment of resources.

Step 6: Action required is where you reveal how you would use the concentration of resources/forces, surprise/deception, and mobility; ratio planning; and understand the use of Combat Power versus Manpower.

1. Location of Existing Friendly Bases that must be maintained.
2. What additional bases must be established, purpose, time-distance?
3. Determine how the bases contribute to the main task/objective.

Category 3: BLT

Step 7: Broad Concept and Impacts is where you look at the strategic, operational, impacts to tactical mission accomplishment.

1. Show forces and how they fit into broad strategic picture and other theaters.

Step 8: Logistics is where you determine the logistics requirements and capabilities by determining the Operational/Logistical Requirements and conduct a Force Flow Analysis of planned moved using a Timed-Phased Force Deployment Database (TPFDD) and finally conduct War

Gaming to consider "What If"
scenarios to build agility in your plan.

1. Determine the Production capability necessary to achieve national objectives. (Time)
2. What is the lag time between plan and execution in months, weeks?
3. What is the lag time between plan and execution for EN in months, weeks?
4. What is the time-table for production of key supplies, Class I, V, III, forces, transportation, etc.?
5. Do you need rapid acceleration or long drawn-out attrition war?
6. Can you provide what is needed given one of the above timelines?
7. Does this contribute to a short or longer war?

Step 9: Total Analysis and Assessment is where you assess if the plan is feasible.

Analysis:

1. Are you approaching in a logical manner with production greatly accelerated to win?
2. Is the will of the people/nation behind you?
3. Are you beating the EN in resupplying your fighting forces?
4. Are your production levels being met by industry capability?

Assessment:

1. Strategic Employment of forces by nation and their ability to reinforce and probable actions?
2. Based on assumptions, what is the outcome based on actions needed to be taken?
3. Action needed: Overwhelming forces, surprise, mobility, speed, reserves.
4. Latest information on military strength and capacities looking at ratios/ratio planning?
5. Give all what is it believed it would take to achieve the objective, strategy, approach.
6. What are any indicators of departure from success?
7. Can you effectively visualize the battlefield landscape?
8. Where are the bottlenecks, shipping, rail, transportation facilities, MHE, storage?

9. What will it take in men, equipment in STONs?
10. How long will it take to achieve what is needed to take begin execution?

These nine steps will help you determine if your if your plan is supportable by the subtle influences that will allow you to use intuitive judgment to make rapid, better plans.

SPIRAL-BASED THINKING 5

The endstate of FORCE FIELD
WIZARDRY is to enhance your visibility
while simplifying the parts to the whole;
with the goal of optimizing decisions that
leads to sustained readiness. To achieve
this state, you must be able to see the
whole network from end-to-end and place
sensors within the network at key points to
be able to track and monitor supplies and
services as they are requested and sourced.
You must first start by asking what
processes, resources, and requirements are
needed because these three elements are
below the line (denominator) and underpin
understanding of FORCE FIELD
WIZARDRY. You must then determine
the plan, what needs to be synchronized,

and monitored above the line (numerator). So, you have 3/3 = 1 Whole.

Processes look at the actions and functions or changes that need to happen from end-to-end. Some examples of functions are contracting, RSOI, deployment/ redeployment, fueling, etc. and how you able to monitor logistics performance to determine what is working and what is not working.

Resources look at the total asset visibility of logistics resources that's in the operating environment that you currently have to work with. This can impact MC, $, Legal, Risks, Critical Events, and supplies and maintenance capabilities. It can also include Host Nation and other Nation capabilities. This total asset visibility must show what's in-transit, storage, sourced, and issued.

Requirements are the bedrock of the network because they determine all other capabilities needed. Requirements can come from anywhere as they determine what is needed to achieve the outcome desired. They determine how those in the network will be tasked or organized. Requirements must be monitored as well because they change over time due to changes in the plan or operational environment. One additional requirement is providing the right information to the different organizations who need them. Key to achieving this is know what they want, why they want it, and where they need it; then report and brief it.

Mapping Spiral-Based Thinking

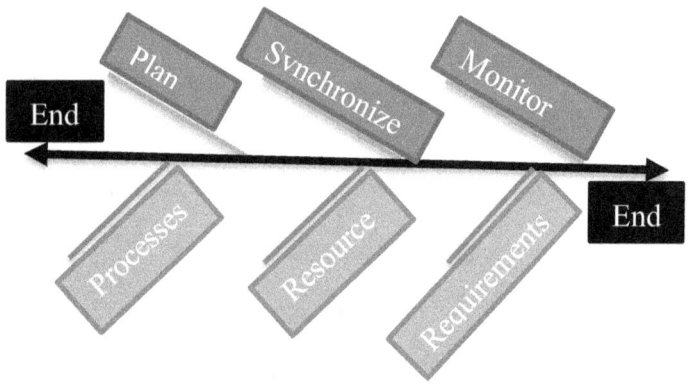

Figure 2 Enhanced Spiral-Based Thinking Map

Now here is what separates the great thinkers from the good thinkers: You must be able to see the **Plan** (system design and planning over phases) and its processes, resources, and requirements. See the **Synchronized** (of resource allocation and execution) of processes, resources, and requirements. And finally, **Monitor** (where you are in the network to be able see what you need to see to effectively and efficiently deliver the products and services at the right place and time) given the processes, resources, and requirements. Key to your success is seeing from the source to the end-user, the shifts in non-linear center of gravity, weighted, as the essential infrastructure and environment changes over time; either expanding, restricting, repositioning, recovering, or simply moving based upon changes in the operational tempo and consumption rates. If you can visualize this end-to-end in your mind, you will be able to provide sustained readiness in any operating environment.

LOGISTICS IPB 6

Battle success depends on your ability to see the battlefield holistically and in parts.

A responsive, balanced distributed Army theater logistic system for sustained land combat is a key ingredient to battlefield success.

In past wars, the logistics system had to be tailored in size, structure, and procedures to support the mission, composition, and concept of operations and that will not change as doctrine changes.

There is no accepted doctrine for the format of a campaign plan to guide logisticians in planning, or requesting intelligence.

Future opponents will not allow the U.S. six-months to prepare for combat and logisticians are still not capable of sustaining the extended phases of campaigns and major operations.

Logistics intelligence is the basis for effective operational level logistics planning and modeling.

In particular, situation development, or intelligence preparation of the battlefield, is the key to operational level planning.

The key question here is, what intelligence does the operational level logistician require when planning theater sustainment, and is it available in a form applicable to the operational level of war?

In this dynamic book you have seen that processes are a vital part of what is required. These processes include the logistics preparation of the theater, creation of the service support plan, design of the balanced distribution plan, and completion of the sustainment estimate.

For optimal logistics planning, Logistic planners must first develop the macro-logistics support plan during the initial development of the campaign plan and then develop the micro-logistics support plan.

Macro-Logistics Support Planning

The macro-logistics support plan consists of Operational intelligence that concentrates on the collection, identification, location, and analysis of strategic and operational centers of gravity, leading to successful attack of the enemy center of gravity as well as protection and sustainment of our own centers of gravity.

Operational Logistics METT-TC

The doctrinal tool that guides the logistic planners' development of a theater logistics system are the factors of METT-TC.

Operational Logistics METT-TC has been defined as the framework for evaluating the logistics plans.

The mission is simply defined as the "Support mission derived from the operation." The enemy is defined as the "Threat to Sustainment operations." Terrain and weather are stated in terms of "Effects on requirements and support methods." The troops are defined as the "Total supporting forces-joint, multinational, civilian, contractors." Time available is conveyed in terms of "Influences support requirements and balanced distribution method. The old definition of METT-TC is obsolete because it does not provide enough detail to be used by the logistics planner at the operational level of war as a doctrinal tool in developing optimal plans.

The operational planning tools in current use are not specifically fitted to the operational logistician as aids in developing a theater logistics system during the planning process.

Mission: Leaders determine the mission through analysis of the tasks assigned. The results of that analysis yield the essential tasks that, together with the purpose of the operation, clearly indicate the action required. From the logistics perspective, the purpose of the mission component of operational METT-TC is to determine the mission tasks, the Army theater logistic provider, and the method of entry into the theater.

There should be a way to integrate identifying operational logistics functions with operational logistics tasks in the form of a synchronization matrix or influence grid.

Now, Intelligence support of sustainment planning primarily comes from two sections of the intelligence estimate and the terrain and weather analyses produced during the IPB process and is key to LIPB.

The intelligence requirements for sustainment planning can be met by merging the concepts of key elements of the influence grid with the considerations in developing an influence grid into a model for operational logistics intelligence.

One can define operational logistics IPB as a trio consisting of critical strategic and operational seaports, airfields, and ground/rail LOCs. In this way, the logistics planner can analyze the environment from three perspectives. Intelligence about the facility's important objectives, as well as the surrounding area, providing details on ports, airfields, roads, etc.

Logistical planners required intelligence pertinent to establishing a sustainment base: concerns are primarily accessibility to sea and air lift, storage and transshipment capacities, and accessibility to inland lines of communication that are necessary to develop a concept for establishing subsequent support bases.

In planning the securing of the initial base, and support of subsequent operations, intelligence about port access, transshipment and storage capabilities, and lines of communication must be obtained. The logistics reach of the tactical and operational sustainment bases is determined by visualizing the placement of logistics bases throughout the communications zone and the combat zone.

One must determine what intelligence is available can contribute to planning the five functional systems of the sustainment system: transportation, maintenance, supply, personnel, and health services. The denominator to all these five functions is balanced distribution. The first element we will look at is the Time-Phased Force and Deployment Data Model.

Time-Phased Force and Deployment Data from the Joint Operations Planning System.

Operational logisticians must understand force generation and force flow planning, command and control planning, security planning, and exercise design and how they affect logistics bases design, development, and LOC security. The lack of LOC security planning and the unexpected presence of the enemy can cause major problems if one fails to modify plans in order to protect logistic bases and supply lines.

One can use Augmentation forces to bridge this gap. Augmentation forces are those forces that can be transferred from a supporting organization to the combatant commander or to the operational control of a supported commander. Analysis conducted to determine the troops and support required for mission accomplishment is actually logistics force adapting to project relative combat power and sustain military operations.

Beyond the Logistics Reach

Now, the focus of the logistics planners has been on establishing a logistics system for sustaining the initial footprint. The lack of thorough planning in support of branches and sequels resulted in logistics culmination and operational logistics pauses, which are common events in war experiences. One of the weaknesses of logistics has been a failure of transportation for the support of the subsequent phases of operations.

A more responsive Army theater logistic system for sustained operations uses the seven logistics principles, where responsiveness is the most essential, and all other considerations are irrelevant if the logistics system cannot support be responsive. The operational logistics provider determines the logistics responsiveness of the theater by building a flexible theater logistics system that would require a logistics plan that is simple; port-to-logistics base, logistics base-to-forward or subsequent bases.

Estimate logistics requirements and supporting theater stockage levels determine how to build supporting sustainment force structure. In determining the location of operational and tactical sustainment bases, estimate the logistic reach of the operational logistics bases, one must layout sustainment units on the logistics map to determine capabilities over time and phases. This reveals the time factor in logistics planning. Time Available – One must analyze time in terms of the startup costs to: RSOI combat forces, sustain combat forces, and redeploy combat forces. This leads to micro-logistics planning.

Micro-Logistics Support Planning

The micro-logistics support plan is the technical, quantitative sustainment planning that produces the detailed concept of support and distribution plan requirements. From these requirements, one can infer that the logistic planners will hold planning sessions and be responsible for the entire planning actions and processes.

These processes include the logistics preparation of the theater, creation of the service support plan, design of the distribution plan, and completion of the sustainment estimate.

During campaign planning, the distribution management plan is a key element in a theater's operational logistics concept.

In order to develop the theater distribution plan, logistic planners must have knowledge of distribution concepts, materiel management, and supporting Standard Army Management Information System such as the Battle Command Sustainment Support System. These tools reveal the logistics constraints and finding solutions to logistics constraints is the art of optimal logistics planning.

Logistics commanders and staffs can develop effective campaign plans that provide the optimum level of support to the maneuver commanders both during individual phases or operations and for the duration of the campaign. The supported commander may determine the support priorities for individual logistics organizations.

The logistics organization now must balance direction and flow from the higher logistics commander, requests from supported units, his own estimates, and potential direction from higher echelon maneuver commanders.

Effective planning enables logisticians to anticipate requirements, and validate, synchronize and integrate them with available resources to minimize duplication of effort, resolve shortfalls, mitigate risk and ensure effective support of the Combatant Commander requirements. Through effective logistics planning, leaders are able to support required operations and accomplish the assigned tasks.

This is done primarily by Military Decision-Making Process (MDMP) - a method of planning for Army operational level staffs. The outcome of MDMP is that the commander understands the environment in which he operates, identifies problems to be addressed, determines the actions most appropriate to address those problems, and describes how the command will implement those actions. The goal is to get the commander see Critical Campaign Information Requirements (CCIR) Triggers.

Traditional CCIR, drives a decision commander while campaign CCIR triggers reframing of the commander's understanding of the environment to see that they are align with the intent and campaign approach.

AI THINKING 7

This chapter searches for a **special logistics doctrine, FORCE FIELD WIZARDRY,** that introduces a new **Artificial Intelligent Military Decision-Making Process (aiMDMP)** framework of campaign design elements that can be used to examine how the minimum operational logistics support is key and integrated into operations, and to what degree the tailoring of design elements influenced the level of logistic support in complex environments.

At the campaign operation planning level, logistics can become the dominate factor in determining the proportion of objectives, tempo, and the nature of the operations.

The ability of the theater logistics system to receive, or move forward the assets may affect the entry size and flow of combat force, or determine the instinctual rhythm/timing of operations.

The innovative solutions to resolve operational sustainment and depth of operations ensures that the scheme of operational maneuver is significantly affected by the scheme of logistics support and gaps.

We will see how both operations and logistics instinctually enabled each other to achieve the theater objectives.

Operational logistics provides for maintaining forces and equipment essential to conducting operations that accomplish national policies.

Operational logistics may require the performance of a proportion or all of the sustainment functions.

To measure the effectiveness of operational logistics in war and to challenge the theory of the subordination of logistics, the elements of the design framework provides a basis for considerations in combining logistics into the planning process for future operations.

Emphasizing the links between operational logistics, instinctual intelligence, surveillance, and reconnaissance (I^2SR), and deception design elements of campaigns to determine when to begin and shift intra-theater lines of communications and movements of logistics bases is the key foundation to a special logistics doctrine. Logistics bases should be in-line with the orderly flow, time-phased buildup of logistics support to tactical operations. Effective support is key here instead of focusing on efficient support. A push system of supplies will do until a pull system of supply can be established. Key to success here is to realize that the bases will be established using standards based on the expected duration of use to minimize cost and time. The mission of the unit, how long the unit will be located there, and culture of the services are taken into account. Storage space and available Material Handling Equipment (MHE)/ Trucks should be critically tracked.

The effective use of intra-theater LOCs between the port and the interior lines, paired with the destruction of intermediate basing zones and forced relocation of rear basing areas, enables instinctual, responsive logistics resupply operations in support of forces while restricting the ability for the enemy to adequately provision its forces over untenable LOCs.

To hide the logistics efforts, the concept of **space and sea-based logistic** base development is needed to support Multi-Domain Operations and the doctrine thereafter.

Throughout operations, logistics is integrated into the concept of the operations, and can prove to be the foundation for the successful planning and execution of the war.

Because of the pressing need to conduct security operations, combat forces, with limited support capability, normally deploys before many of the logistics units.

Operational logistics, through support to various campaign design elements, supported the operations taking place in different environments.

Throughout operations logistics must be integrated into the concept of the operations for the successful planning and execution of the war. Operational logistics provides additional capability and can dictate when actions begin.

The limited ground lines of communication and the distances the combat forces moved away from the in-country sustainment locations placed a premium on transportation assets and can lead to the construction of logistic bases: Another factor is that the concept of operations remained the focal point for the integration of all logistical operations.

Second, defensive operations create a reduced pace in operations and allows the operational logistics structure to overcome shortfalls in the reception capability of the theater.

From an operational logistics point of view, since logistics operations may become the focus for operations, it is reasonable to expect instinctive intelligence efforts to become more interested in logistics operations.

The military logistics operations support plan will probably dictate whether its operations is successful.

On the contrary, two such issues remain clear: providing logistics support to force projection platforms and supporting future joint and combined operations.

Further, there is evidence supporting the assertion that the operational environment, and the resulting influence on various campaign design elements, had an effect on the logistics support provided, though these factors affected the execution of this **level of logistics**, not the function itself.

System of inner lines, enabled by increased logistics support at the port coupled with the annihilation of the intermediate and rear basing zones lines of communications untenable and unable to support frontline forces.

The systematic use of inner lines between the port and the river line, paired with the destruction of intermediate basing zones and forced relocation of rear basing areas, enabled responsive logistics resupply operations in support of forces while restricting the ability for the enemy to sufficiently support its forces over shaky LOCs.

The observations of operational logistics in different environments, as evidenced by the degree of integration and influence in the selected campaign design elements, appear to indicate a need for a **special logistics doctrine**. Thus, we introduce:

Artificial Intelligent Military Decision-Making Porcess (aiMDMP) in Algorithmic Warfare that pulls coherent data and information so that a person can actually think about what they are seeing and extract some type of decision.

aiMDMP looks to instinctively automate processes wherever possible using AI. It involves creative anticipatory thinking about the problem and not getting bogged down with tedious work sifting through exponential and spatial amounts of information looking for aggregate and targetable data is the ultimate goal.

It will allow you to wage successful campaigns against large conventionally-armed states and their militaries, against widely dispersed terrorists, and everything in between-generally at great distances from our shores in the most dispersed areas in the world.

More rapidly and deeper, the **aiMDMP** will exploit man-machine and artificial intelligence interface to enhance performance, for clearer guidance and direction by embracing technology to enable **degrees of freedom of movement** on the battlefield.

An aiMDMP, known as FORCE FIELD WIZARDRY, will balance future capabilities and leverage cyber, information, and artificial intelligence enabling flexibility, agility, and freedom of movement between the five domains of space, cyber, air, land, and maritime.

Developing an analytically based wargaming process, and leveraging commercial technological advances of hybrid logistics, operations in the information environment, and Expeditionary Advanced Base Operations. Artificial Intelligence, as a discipline, is the study of systems that act in a way that would appear to be intelligent. It will allow automated operational planning in response to an emerging crisis based on the ability to influence outcomes.

With increase of artificial intelligence in societal applications, artificial intelligence technologies can aid in decision-making beyond intelligent mission command systems by use of instinctive cognitive computing.

Instinctive Cognitive Computing - Systems that learn at scale or proportion, reason with purpose, and interact with humans naturally using various tailorable artificial intelligence technologies.

There are Hard AI / General AI - Artificial Intelligence systems capable of exhibiting apparently intelligent behavior at least as advanced as a human across a broad range of thinking tasks.

There are also Soft AI / Narrow AI - Artificial Intelligence systems capable of successfully completing simple or highly specific use.

Instinctive Artificial intelligence is a holistic concept encompassing a variety of technical capabilities that correspond to intelligence.

General artificial intelligence would operate as a subsystem of a larger system, performing systematic narrow AI tasks.

Artificial Intelligence, as a discipline, is the study of systems that act in a way that would appear to be intelligent or intelligent-like.

Technical system can perform highly thinking functions as well or better than humans.

While private industry continues to pursue and push the limits of artificial intelligence, internationally, this dynamic provides the unintended opportunity for the military to maximize its planning capacity using instinctive artificial intelligence.

These systems employ instinctive artificial intelligence at a level above the operational level, denying their employment to tactical planners.

While these systems are useful, they merely provide situational awareness and **not the task automation intended for instinctive artificial intelligence system**.

Without instinctive artificial intelligence systems at the higher echelons, the Multi-

Domain Task Force staff will be unable to keep pace with synchronizing operations.

Within the context of instinctive artificial intelligence, the **pairing of an artificial mind and human mind** is the concept.

Just as mission command systems are prepared and assimilated during the capability step, **aiMDMP**, the artificial intelligence system, would be provided a combined data set consisting of higher headquarters operations order/annexes with sub-step directions 1 & 3, 5, & 8, 13…of Mission Analysis for straight forward integrating of instinctive artificial intelligence.

Instinctive Intelligence Preparation of the Battlefield is the systematic process of analyzing the mission variables of enemy, terrain, weather, and civil considerations to determine their effect on operations for both enemy and friendly forces. Instinctive Logistical Preparation of the Battlefield is the systematic process of analyzing the mission variables of strategic chokepoints, LOCs, and their influences on the operation scheme of maneuver and determining key decision points. Remember that decision points are usually geographic, such as a sea-lane, a town, airfield, or boundaries, airspace. They indicate a point at which one must determine the best use of available resources and weigh that use against risk.

Higher headquarters' operations orders and commander's guidance/intent inform a unit's mission, making the mission statement systematic and thus calculable by an instinctive artificial intelligence program.

The instinctive artificial intelligence technologies of today have not demonstrated the ability to determine courses of action, taking into account the level of detail required to plan fires, synchronize intelligence assets, and arrange movement formations.

This requires continued development of instinctive knowledge enabled logistics through our continued work with the Services, the United States Transportation Command, the Army Materiel Command, the United States Joint Forces Command, and the Defense Logistics Agency on implementing the Logistics Enterprise Architecture, and with additional tools such as Radio Frequency Identification Tags and Unique Identification in support of **aiMDMP** using **FORCE FIELD WIZARDRY** technologies.

So consciously make it a point to think this way until you can simply do it without thinking and you will experience much success in becoming a master of filtering information using these steps to concentrate strategic thinking:

Sequence 1: You first **Ask** the most important questions at all times…**Am I doing the right thing, things right, and where are the center or pillar, essential meaning, and purpose of what I'm seeing**?

Sequence 2: Seek the many connections/relationships and different ways (perspectives) by looking around you, paying attention to what you see, know, and do now and expect to see, know, do to influence the future.

Sequence 3: Know: Seeing the meaning of places, people, and things while grasping the grand drama requires imagination based on seeing levels and expectations. Wisdom will be developed by instinctively judging what right action to take, based on knowledge, insight, experience, common sense, and understanding to see things differently, more broadly, and deeply.

You must **MEASURE** all that you do. That is, you must be sure of what actions to take because you have calculated and then can anticipate the outcome. Be able to see the extreme ends of a problem or question and then ask if time is a critical factor in solving or answering it. Determine the worth, authorities, and rewards.

Listen for the subtle connections that are shown by pain levels, desire, honor, and any new information that comes to mind and then act on it until you meet with success.

Dinosaurs have long disappeared from the Earth, but the butterfly remains. What is the secret to its ability to endure? I believe that now that you understand and can apply the triggers and indicator tools presented in this book, you can live a long successful life no matter the change that is around you.

I know that after reading this eye-opening, hands-on book, you now know how to integrate and control any environment by learning how to use concentrated, guided thinking to sense how to increase the velocity of resources across time and space, in the right amount, at the right place, to identify tradeoffs and risks in chaotic environments.   Yes, the eye is the secret of it all, because the eye sees what's in Its range. It sees nothing or everything. You also will use the contents of this book as a guide to use when you need to make course corrections as you navigate by using sensors to help transform objective foundations of thought; which is based on mathematics like calculus, trigonometry, and geometry. Now, you will be able to analyze and sort out what's important and interesting as you put things into context, see new insights, and anticipate trends. You finally see that that center of gravity is a continuous process throughout events and that center of gravity can change during the course of an event and may not be apparent or readily discernible.

This rare book you've read provided insights and original ideas for you as a sharper thinker on how to be a master intellect and creative-anticipatory genius. These underpinning tools will integrate and control any environment by guiding your thinking to sense how to increase the velocity of resources across time and space in the right amount at the right place while reducing risks and embarrassing delays.

This timeless book has provided comprehensive and sound underpinning tools and now you have them; for they lead to the answers to how to think exponentially when trying to sense and determine what's important now and in the future that will lead to less redundancies and risk and produce greater successes as you think from a longer and sharper perspective. You can now began creatively seizing the initiative with awareness, foresight, timing, and imagination.

Still further, this comprehensive book you have read indeed provided insights for mastering the art of FORCE FIELD WIZARDRY by using a strategy of layered/relational networked geometry/spatial projection of forces and fluid flow distribution that allows exponential growth in flexibility, precision, and coordination to anticipate and be imaginative in any environment.
Now, the driving theme for this stunning book is the question, **how to leverage**

FORCE FIELD WIZARDRY at the cutting-edge of success? We answered that question in a profound way in this book. FORCE FIELD WIZARDRY consist of three areas that was discussed throughout this superb book:

(1) Hold the necessary sight alignment and make adjustments to grasp the situation

(2) See a number of positions and instantly judge all the advantages from known positions

(3) Master of non-linear time, space, and mass (concentration)

The answer to the driving theme for this wise book is that yes, width always at the expense of knowing processes and underpinnings, and the good news is that you can integrate and control any environment by attuning your mind to the unconscious and using your imagination and It (Instinct) to guide your thinking, sensing how to increase the velocity of resources across time and space in the right amount at the right place and be able to collect reports and brief what you see.

You have seen FORCE FIELD WIZARDRY and are now thinking at a non-linear triangulated-wizard level...but remember and know this secret, life is an art, strategy and timing is key to success in life, and there is always another level to It.

ABOUT THE AUTHOR

He's known as one of the world's unified thinkers and founder of a breakthrough thinking method called Context Thinking. He is also the founder of *The Black Chair Series*.

A 10-year veteran of the context thinking field, Joseph Graham is unique among experts as the man who's actually developed and executed the day-to-day thinking strategies.

Today, he's the #1 best selling author of *Master The Art of Context Thinking, The 11 Golden Principles of*

Context Thinking, The Game of Life and Its Lessons, Thinking Quadrant: How to Think on Your Feet Even When You're Sitting, Blockchain Thinking, Master of the Situation, and many others, published worldwide.

Other information can be found at http://jgrahamenterprises.wixsite.com/one pagebooks

Check out our newest product offering: "One Page Books". We help you save time by providing you exactly what you need to answer questions at the right time. You can subscribe starting at $1 per month. You get a minimum of 12 great books per year.

BONUS NOTES:

Fundamentals of Original Smart Planning /Thinking

Planning/Thinking can be relatively easy or hard. It can be easy for some or hard and hopeless for others. Easy seems to follow the path of least resistance to understand. Planning/thinking relies on basic principles and rules of thumbs that point to a line of thought.

Experience and principles solve tough problems to get to the essence of right planning/thinking. This book is about learning how to think and listen to get to the right solution by seeing the right insight and in the right conditions. Right insight results in harmony and less effort.

Planners/Thinkers can become addicted to formula gained by years of trial and error. Position, Control, and Sense of a thing are vital components of planning/thinking. It is easier to follow a well-warned path than to do original planning/thinking. Second-hand information is easier than first-hand information, but second-hand information develops your ability to judge things less and in correcting flawed reasoning. The more you use second-hand information, the less likely you will do any original thinking, and if you don't use it, like they say, you lose it.

What planners/thinkers need is the ability to judge things. But what is judgment and how do you develop judgement?

Judgment is the ability to make reliable,

right decisions/conclusions based upon a mental picture of what is ideal/right base upon experience. Judgments are formed from past experiences, good and bad, loud and quiet, up and down, ease and effort/tension. You can become better at planning/thinking if you develop your ability to reliably judge things. If you do, you will get away from learning that is relying on the law of probabilities/gambling. You become good a planning/thinking by practice. The difference between a pro an amateur is preparation. With preparation, you will be able to do more than others and navigate in any environment without less doubt and uncertainty.

You must operate from the right position in the right environment. These two conditions, position and environment is the foundation no matter what other elements change around you. Concentrate on these two and you can improve your planning/thinking to make effective decisions with ease. Right thinking is the path to success no matter what comes your way. You have to learn to think for yourself. This is something you develop yourself at your pace. You develop it until you can see and feel your way ahead with ease and without effort while being in control of the situation.

The next key is your imagination. You must use your judgment, experience, and thoughts to control your imagination. Directed, controlled imagination is the source of all the discoveries of the hidden forces of nature. Without imagination, you will have little chance of success. Imagination is formed from images, concepts, and feelings; what you see, think about, and feel. You must be able to see, think, and feel a situation that is in harmony with all three aspects. This is the perfect harmonic balance that all are striving to achieve and that we all know exists, that is why we desire to achieve it. To get there we must learn how to listen and train ourselves to hear what it is before us and imagine what is beyond us. Think big and wide and you will be able to achieve more. If you want to think better, you have to do the things that make you think better. You must develop your ability to be a sight-reader of environments and the elements in the environment; whole to the parts, and parts to the whole to master planning/thinking. Great planners/thinkers live in the playground of their imagination. Do not be afraid to change your mind; a wise man will change his mind and share knowledge.